The Championship Formula

WINNING IN EVERY POSSIBLE AREA OF YOUR LIFE **WITH YOUR FISTS UP!**

JOEY GILBERT

Traitmarker Books

Franklin | TN

The

Championship

Formula

WINNING IN EVERY POSSIBLE AREA
OF YOUR LIFE **WITH YOUR FISTS UP!**

JOEY GILBERT

Copyright ©2022 by Joey Gilbert
All rights reserved.

No part of this book may be used or reproduced by any means: graphic, electronic, or mechan-
ical, including photocopying, recording, taping, or by any information storage retrieval system
without the written permission of the author except in the case of brief quotations embodied in
critical articles and reviews. Because of the dynamic nature of the Internet, any web addresses
or links contained in this book may have changed since publication and may no longer be valid.
Although every precaution has been taken to verify the accuracy of the information contained
herein, the author and publisher assume no responsibility for any errors or omissions so that no
liability is assumed for damages that may result from the use of the information contained within. The views expressed in this work are solely those of the author and do not necessarily reflect
the views of the publisher whereby the publisher hereby disclaims any responsibility for them.

BOOK PUBLISHING INFORMATION
Traitmarker Books
2984 Del Rio Pike
Franklin, TN 37069
traitmarkerbooks.com
traitmarker@gmail.com

ATTRIBUTIONS
Editors: Sharilyn Grayson, Warren Gilbert
Cover Design: Robbie Grayson III
Cover Photo:

PUBLICATION DATA
Paperback ISBN: 978-1-64921-547-5
Hardcover ISBN: 978-1-63752-167-0

Interior Title & Text Font: Minion Pro
Interior Text Font: Minion Variable Concept
Interior Title Fonts: Ink Free

Printed in the United States of America.

To my CHAMPION daughter Aiella:
My saving grace. My motivation
to fight for humanity.

TABLE OF CONTENTS

Introduction | i

SECTION 1 | COMMUNITY

SECTION 2 | HEALTH

Section 3 | Ambition

Section 4 | Motivation

SECTION 5 | POSITIVITY

Introduction
What is *The Championship Formula?*

Everyone holding this book in your hands right now, I want to thank you sincerely for taking the time to listen to my story. My name is Joey Gilbert, and I want to discuss with you what I call *The Championship Formula.* I have spent my life perfecting this formula, which has given me great success and happiness. I'm sharing my story with you right now because I want everyone who will listen to experience the kind of blessed life I enjoy.

Let me ask you a few things before I introduce myself. *What's your biggest challenge? What steps have you taken towards success so far? Are you a champion?*

That last question is especially important. A champion will do what it takes to win. Muhammad Ali said "I don't count my sit-ups. I only start counting when it starts hurting, because they're the only ones that count. That's what makes you a champion."

So Muhammad Ali tells me that a champion never quits. I believe that principle. I can give you *The Championship Formula,* but it will only work for you if you apply it with the same kind of heart and will as Ali. You have to go at it with that never-quit determination if it's going to help you win.

See, that's the secret. You have to determine deep within yourself that you are a champion before you can do the things that champions do. So make that determination now. I'm serious.

Decide that you can win, and then I'll show you how to do it.

The "how" behind *The Championship Formula* has its roots in my life story. I'm from Chicago, but I moved with my family to Reno, NV at a young age. On a dare I joined the boxing team in college and became a national champion. I was an undefeated boxer in college, winning three back-to-back NCAA national boxing championships, the Nevada State Golden Gloves champion, four-time All American, as well as the WBC-USNBC & WBO-NABO middleweight champion with a combined professional record of 21-3 with 17 KOs.

Now I'm an attorney with my own firm who has recently filed lawsuits to open Nevada back up for business. You can view that work at joeygilbert.com. I was also an entrepreneur in the cannabis realm, a community advocate, an event promoter, a youth trainer, and the owner of Joey Gilbert Real Estate. Additionally, after a ten-year legal battle, I am now officially a co-owner of the National Gold Mine and a principle in the Hygrade Gold, Ltd. company.

I adopted the champion mentality early in adulthood, but refining the way to use my determination and optimism has taken the last two decades. Now I can take that life experience and bring it to you with *The Championship Formula.* I'm going to share with you how to be a CHAMP:

COMMUNITY—Nothing happens in a vacuum. If you want to win at life, you have to surround yourself with people who support you as a winner. Now life gave you one set of people around you, and those people may or may not be contributing to your success. If they're not, go find people who do. You need that community.

HEALTH—Your health is your number one tool for achievement. Yes, you need a strong body, no matter what you want to do with your life or how particularly you want to win. You also need a strong mind, a flexible heart, an ethical soul, and a trained will. The possibility of health exists in all the dimensions where you exist as a person. Get healthy.

AMBITION—Here's that champion mindset. You have to say inside yourself, "I can win, and I am going to win. I'm never going to let anything stand in my way." Devotion to your own welfare is irreplaceable.

MOTIVATION— How do you want to win at life? What is most important to you? Where are you going to direct your time, energy, and determination? You have to answer these questions about your own personal values, and dig deep for the truth of them, if your winning is going to mean anything to you.

Positivity—Life is full of opportunity, and you are uniquely capable of seizing the openings you need in order to do what is important to you. So much good can happen. If you focus on the good that is possible, you will achieve it. You don't have time to waste on being negative.

There you go. That's the *Cliff's Notes* version of *The Championship Formula*. I have a lot to tell you about the way life taught me those principles. So I invite you on a tour of my personal evolution through the rest of the book.

All my fellow champs out there, I salute you. Let's get started.

PART 1
COMMUNITY

"

Everyone has a plan...
until they get punched
in the mouth.

"

MIKE TYSON

1 | Identity

In a lot of ways, the story of my life is the story of a lost kid. The person you are when you're leaving the regulated classroom of childhood for the lawless playground of youth stays with you longer than you would think. And for me, that person was lost.

When I was a kid, I knew who I was. My last name might have been Gilbert, but I was an Italian kid from Chicago. I had friends and extended family (mom's family) who knew me so well I didn't even have to think about getting to know myself.

Also, I'm probably the most ADHD (Attention-Deficit/Hyperactivity Disorder) person you will ever meet. There are some drawbacks to that condition, but there are also some advantages. Living with ADHD means that I learned to work around the drawbacks and rock the hell out of the advantages.

After my third year in high school, my parents took me to a pediatric endocrinologist who tested me. He showed them the baseline charts and then where I was. He basically couldn't graph how ADHD I was. My physical size was three years behind my chronological age. He looked at my Dad with some sympathy and said, "Dr. Gilbert, I don't know if higher education is in the cards for your son."

Luckily, the Lieutenant Colonel didn't take that opinion at face value. He'd always expected me to fulfill his expectations and my true potential. An ADD & ADHD diagnosis wasn't going to change that. I got a prescription for Adderall, which has truly helped me focus ever since then, and I went back to school.

I tell you that story because it helps describe how I interact with the world. I have a ton of restless energy that I've learned to channel into valuable projects now. I'm always thinking of something new I want to try or learn, and I'm usually thinking about a dozen different things at once. Now, being ADD & ADHD means that I'm able to handle wearing a lot of different hats at one time: lawyer, dad, athlete, entrepreneur (and for the last few months, writer).

As a boy, being ADD & ADHD wasn't so helpful because I didn't know what it was or how it affected me. Other people just saw me as a hyper little kid with a smart mouth. I was a hyper little kid, and totally distractable—so distractable that I didn't engage in much introspection until later in my life. That contributed to the lostness I felt and seldom acknowledged to myself.

I didn't want to dwell on any potential flaws. I liked to be the answer—the guy who could get you what you wanted to have or who could find you what you were looking for. That kind of guy—the sharp fixer who was two steps ahead of the muscle—that was a true Chicago stereotype. When I was super small, I was right where I belonged and right where I wanted to be.

Then my mom married a hard-ass Marine, and we moved to Nevada, land of the cowboys. My life would never be the same. And for a long time, I didn't know who to be in it.

2 | **Parents**

I had no idea for a long time that I wasn't a Gilbert by birth. The Lieutenant Colonel, the imposing Marine my mom married before I was two, stepped right into the Dad role in our family as soon as he arrived. There was no "stepdad" nonsense in the Gilbert house. I grew up with a man of the house who drew lines, set expectations, and exacted consequences.

Everybody called the Lieutenant Colonel "the quiet man." He didn't speak often, but when he did, people listened. He wasn't just a Lieutenant Colonel in the Marines— he was a commander of attention and re-spect wherever he went.

You didn't even think about disappointing this guy. If he told me something that needed to be done, it got done one way or the other. Say I was supposed to clean out the garage before I went out with friends on a Friday night—and, also, say that I busted my hump getting that garage in shape, but I didn't quite make the deadline.

Some of you may have grown up with dads who would have put an arm around you and said, "Gee, son, I can see you put a lot of effort into this job. You go have fun, and we'll work on it together Saturday morning."

Good for you.

If I turned up and said, "Dad, I'm really sorry, but I just didn't—"

I wouldn't have gotten any further than that. I might not have gotten that far. Warren Gilbert would hold up a hand, pin me with his eyes, and say, "I don't need a history lesson. Cancel your night." And I would have spent Friday night (and all of Saturday and Sunday as needed) getting the damn garage clean.

Lest you think that Mom married some abusive psycho, let me say right up front that Warren Gilbert is a fair and decent man who typifies the best qualities of his generation. I never doubted that he cared what happened to me and who I turned out to be. He cared so much that it never occurred to me that he wasn't my birth dad.

Being the go-getter I was as a kid, I wanted to work and achieve. The Lieutenant Colonel fully supported my ambitions to stay off my hindquarters and get shit done. That was the kind of son a Marine was supposed to have. So no one in our family thought it was strange that I wanted to get a job in middle school.

But I was young enough that I needed a state-issued ID to show the car wash that was willing to hire me. So Mom drove me to the DMV to get one. She stayed in the car while I went in.

The lady at the counter looked at the documents I handed her and said, "I need your change of name confirmation."

"My what?"

"The documented proof of your legal name change. Your mom will have it."

For the first time, I looked down at my birth certificate and saw that my last name at birth had been Chiarmonte. Warren Gilbert was listed exactly nowhere. I walked out to the car with a whole lot of questions for my mom.

For years, I'd had some half-buried memories that I thought were dreams or imagination. In one scene, I heard my baby voice saying, "Daddy Warren" and "Daddy Joe." In another, I saw a man standing over my mom and sister, yelling at them and making them cry. It was a scary image. I didn't really believe it had happened.

Now I heard that my memories were real, that the man who helped create me biologically had not been a real prince to my mom, and that the man who was performing the dad function in my house with a great degree of enthusiasm was not the guy nature had intended to perform it.

This news rocked me to my core. Along with all of the rootlessness that came from being out of my native city and away from the family and friends I knew, this realization of who I was and who I was not shoved me even further out into the psychic cold. Not only was I a stranger to the people in my school and my city, but I was also a stranger to myself.

I had a real attitude about the cover-up. I started calling Dad "Warren." That did not go over well, but I was past caring. My parents' deception, as kindly as they may have meant it, erased the goodwill the Lieutenant Colonel had earned by showing up every day, treating my mom well, and putting a roof over my head and food in my stomach.

It would take a significant meeting and a shared love to bring me back to the respect I owed my Dad. After several years of us butting heads, me challenging him with less than stellar behavior, and him bringing me back to reality, we reached an understanding and developed an unshakable bond that is steadfast and unwavering. Whether it was coaching me in soccer, being the team physician throughout my high school football days, or being my coach/doctor/corner man throughout my professional boxing career, he has been by my side providing support, guidance, and counsel... and still does. We became a team: Team Gilbert. More about that later.

3 | Siblings

No one else in your life can take the place of a brother or a sister. No one else knows all the memories in your head, and no one else has dealt with your parents the way you have. So no one else can have your back quite like a sibling.

I've got three siblings, all sisters. Gina, born Gina Chiarmonte just a year before yours truly, was my OG sibling. When the Lieutenant Colonel came along, he added a sister nearly Gina's age, Melissa. Then about ten years later, mom and Warren had my sister Anna. But because Melissa lived with us part time and Anna was so much younger, Gina was my closest sister.

Everybody should have a sister like Gina. Generous, smart, and happy, she has an infectious energy. When we were really young, I started calling her Sparkle. The nickname caught on, and to this day, it's her license plate.

Gina cares about people deeply, and there's nothing she wouldn't do for her family. I knew I could always rely on her to listen to me, keep my secrets, and have my back. Yeah, we teased and fought like normal. But I knew deep in my heart that I could trust her with anything.

She's older than I am; so the whole transition from birth dad to the Lieutenant Colonel hit her differently. She remembered how unhappy the Chiarmonte house was, and she saw the change in Mom when Warren Gilbert came on the scene. Those were memories that just weren't conscious in me.

As far as my sister and I were concerned, there were different thoughts and opinions about our two dads. Sis with her understanding and generous heart was fine with meeting Mr. Chiarmonte when he expressed a desire to see us and find out how we were doing. Unfortunately, he had not had any contact with us for fourteen years. It turned out that he was friends with our uncle Scotty and that he'd been right around the corner from Nani and Poppy Aiello our whole lives, every time we'd come to Chicago for Christmas or Easter. Nice.

I, on the other hand, did not want to see this stranger. I had a dad. I was perfectly fine with the dad I had. Yeah, Warren Gilbert and I had hit some rough patches, but I didn't need some guy off the street who had chosen not to meet me for fourteen years waltzing in and congratulating himself for the great person I was. Forget that.

Besides, the sense of menace in my one memory of him troubled me. I wondered whether my toddler memory was flawed, whether I had inherited genes from a seriously bad dude. I figured the further back in my rearview mirror this guy stayed, the better.

But Gina worked on me. It wasn't that she wanted

to meet him so much, but she wanted to please our uncle. And she also felt sorry for Mr. Chiarmonte. It didn't bother her meeting him. Like me, she knew she already had a good dad, but that knowledge didn't make her defensive. It made her generous.

To please Gina, I agreed to the meeting. Since it was happening, I came up with my own agenda for the conversation. I wanted to ask Joe Chiarmonte why he'd left me. I wanted to know why he hadn't kept in touch—why I'd never gotten a phone call or a birthday card from him. I wanted a reason for the rejection I sensed.

Next time the family went back to Chicago, our extended family hit on a plan for us to meet him. We were all staying with Nani and Poppy Aiello, and they invited Mr. Chiarmonte to come over and pick us up to take us out to dinner. Mom headed upstairs and made Warren go with her because everyone thought Mr. Chiarmonte might find him threatening. I guess he would have.

I sat at the restaurant table and fumed. Gina made conversation. I noted the ways I looked like him. But I knew I would never act like him. My temper rose and rose.

Mr. Chiarmonte could go down on his knees and beg for my forgiveness. He could tell me how much he'd missed me and how much he regretted staying away from me all these years. He could argue for me to come and live with him. He could promise to make up for all the time he'd missed. It wouldn't matter.

I felt no connection, no ease. Family is supposed to make you feel at home, right? You're supposed to feel a deep connection to family that sets you at ease. You don't have to pretend around your family. You can be yourself.

You're not supposed to break into a flop sweat and flounder around to cover strained silences. You're not supposed to wring out your brain for something to say. You're not supposed to want the night to be over.

Despite the weirdness, I asked birth dad my most pressing questions. *Why had he stayed away? Why didn't I know him? Why was there this Chiarmonte-shaped hole in my life?*

And surprise, surprise—he didn't have a good answer. At least not one that satisfied me.

Basically, he repeated what my mom had explained. He thought he was doing what was best for me. He didn't want me to be confused. Warren Gilbert was going to be there daily, doing dad things. Joe didn't want me to wonder why he wasn't there doing dad things instead.

I could only stand so much of those mealy-mouthed excuses before I lost my cool. I made my displeasure and dissatisfaction abundantly clear. I stood up and left the restaurant. I went to a pay phone and called my Poppy to come and pick me up.

From then on, we saw him from time to time when we went back home to Chicago. Those meetings were never my idea, and they were never enough to soothe my anger. I could not understand this man, and I was beginning to suspect that I just didn't want to try.

You know who stuck with me in the middle of that blown-to-smithereens evening? You know who was with me on the streets of Chicago while I walked off my anger and disappointment? My sister.

You can disagree about a lot of things and wound each other in a lot of ways, but your siblings are the ones who are there for you. Even when they can't make anything any better, they can understand. They can be there. They can walk home with you, even when you're still figuring out what home means.

4 | **Nation of Immigrants**

I believe that names mean things, and I know that my own name means a lot to me. It explains me to myself in a lot of ways. Maybe when you see how my name informs my life story, you'll be inspired to reexamine your own name for the meanings that were intended and those you've forged by your actions.

Let's start with Joseph. This is clue number one that I come from a Catholic family: I was named for the adopted father of Jesus. But not only does it nod to my religious heritage, it also nods to my own adoption by the man who raised me. What Joseph did for Jesus, Warren did for me. The story of adoption and fostering is strong within me from the start.

Also, Joseph means "he shall add" in Hebrew. I look at that meaning and see the drive deep within me to expand my areas of influence, to do more, to achieve more. Like the Joseph who went down to Egypt, I've been betrayed and suffered from false accusations. Like that same Joseph, I've risen above the slander to rule my corner of the world.

My middle name is Salvatore. That name unpacks a whole history of strong, principled Italian warriors that eventually produced me. It's a history I'm proud to own and a family that I'm proud to claim.

Way back in the Middle Ages, there were three brothers. One became a priest, another a lawyer, and the third became a warrior. Guess which branch my bloodline hailed from? That's right: warrior all the way back!

I saw this kind of culture in my Italian neighborhood back in Chicago. Even as a child, I felt the values of personal courage, family loyalty, and the importance of honor. They're lessons I'm happy to claim as part of my Salvatore heritage.

Besides, the name literally means "savior", and though I am by no means anybody's eternal savior, I do see in my daily work that I save people in practical ways. I help DUI offenders and domestic abuse complainants take a second look at how they're living and turn things around. I fight bad guys in court sometimes and win justice for hurting people. Lately, I've been able to save business owners from government overreach. I value this work deeply.

Now, my birth name, Chiarmonte, has been a bit of a mystery. It doesn't show up in a lot of databases. As best I can tell, it comes from *sera* which is *evening*, and *mantiene* which means *keeps*. So it's *one who keeps the evening*—like a night watchman. Like Batman in medieval Italian! I take it to mean that I come from people who keep the peace, people who keep others safe while they sleep.

This meaning, too, applies to the work I do. It also applies to who I am on a deep level. I feel that deep need to protect those around me, to keep them safe and see them through to lighter times.

Now the really interesting thing is that all this other history got mixed with Gilbert history when Mom married the Lieutenant Colonel. And here is what being a Gilbert means.

The name Gilbert comes from the medieval practice of fostering. Yep, the idea of a replacement parent is built straight into the language! You see, the nobility in Europe wanted to build strong ties with each other and to share knowledge. So when a boy was old enough to part with his parents, he'd be sent to another castle to learn how to be a knight and a noble.

These other nobles who fostered him would teach him swordplay, virtue, and horsemanship, as well as educate him in astronomy, mathematics, history, and religion. The foster parents got a servant and a future ally. The better job they did molding this kid, the more valuable the ally they could call on when the kid inherited the estate from his parents.

This whole idea of fostering makes sense of my relationship with the Lieutenant Colonel. In my early life, while I was developing values and deciding who I wanted to be, Warren Gilbert poured discipline and motivation into my life experience. He made sure that the man who would emerge would be a strong future ally.

And that's what we are today. I know that I can count on him for advice and support. He knows he can count on me for anything he needs. Because Warren

Gilbert stayed the course, took me in, and treated me as a son, he reaps the benefits now of having me as a faithful ally.

I'm a helper who expands territory. I'm both a Chiarmonte and a Gilbert. And I would not change a thing about either of those identities. They work together to make me who I am.

5 | Friends

I learned the value of friendship through loss. You truly never know how much someone means to you until you don't see them anymore. I got a first lesson, which was painful enough, and then I got the big lesson, the hammer drop, the one that knocked me flat.

The first lesson I got in losing friendship was at the time of the big move from Chicago to Reno. I lost a whole network of cousins and neighbors and friends that meant a lot to me. When I was a small boy there in the neighborhood where my grandparents lived, I never felt alone. Someone was always up to something and inviting me along. I didn't have to wonder what I was doing that day or stare at the four walls of my house and wish something would happen.

No—all I had to do was step out my front door, and I'd join the constant motion, the perpetual games, the party that was happening somewhere. Life was all around me, and I was part of it. I never had to make anything happen. I never had to try to meet anyone. That childhood full of belonging and entertainment was such a gift to me.

When we moved to Reno, it wasn't just that I didn't have a circle of friends and cousins ready made to accept me. It was that people lived differently. They didn't hang out on their front stoops or drop in on each other for dinner spontaneously. The kids in the new neighborhood out west weren't one rowdy pack who were just as welcome in one front yard or open kitchen as another.

Things in Reno were at the same time more and less formal. For instance, my Dad coached my soccer team in an effort to get me exercise and friends at one time. That's a Marine for you: efficient! He got to know the other parents of kids on the team. We also got to know parents at church and from school. Without fail, after the initial introductions, the parents would invite me to call them by their first names. "Call me Bill!" a dad would grin. "Call me Sandy!" a mom would enthuse.

That just felt wrong! I'd been raised to call these people Mr. and Mrs. Whoever They Were. I couldn't just pop out with a Bill or a Sandy. Aside from risking my mom losing her mind, it just felt weird and too familiar. I knew people in the old neighborhood who had changed my diapers and spanked my ass for getting into mischief whose first names were still a complete mystery to me. See? Reno was way less formal that way.

But at the same time, you had to schedule a dinner or a party three weeks out with Bill and Sandy instead of just showing up around dinner and being invited in and treated like royalty. You had to ring the front doorbell and ask if a kid could play instead of just hollering at the back or walking straight in past the mom in the kitchen, who would ask you how your mom and aunts and grandmas were doing. So, in that way, Reno was way more formal.

It was hard as a kid to learn the rules and fit in with everybody else, especially as small as I was. I had a hormone thing that kept me a good three years behind other kids in physical development. When I was nine, I looked six. When I was twelve, I looked nine. And I was in classes and on teams with kids that may have been twelve but looked fourteen. Making friends was hard when I felt like an outsider, and a shrimpy outsider at that.

Also, I just missed the old neighborhood and the people there. Sure, I saw them every Christmas and Easter, but it wasn't the same. They had months' worth of fights and scandals and remembered games and pranks that I had not been there to know at the time. All that shared history drifted over our early connections like snow. At first, I could shovel it away for those visits. Then, after years had passed, too much had built up for me to make a dent. It was nobody's fault, but I was iced out. I lost those friends. I hated how that felt.

My friend circle shrank from a large one to a few guys that liked me for me. One of those guys was DJ Bernardis. We went to school together, first at Our Lady of the Snows and then at Bishop Manogue, and because we lived pretty close, our parents carpooled.

We spent early mornings for years munching toast and tying shoes in each other's parent's cars. We dealt with sibling issues, his and mine, in that cramped space. And we learned our different parents' parenting styles. DJ understood me and my family in a way few people ever did because of those rides back and forth to school.

The friendship overflowed into school and after school, too. DJ was someone who was always up for a bike ride or a race or just messing around in the yard with a ball. He went to the same birthday parties and skating nights as I did. We played on the same teams and suffered through the same parent-teacher nights.

So, DJ was kind of family. He felt like a little bit of the old neighborhood. His parents were Mr. and Mrs. Holmes, and I could yell for him at his back door.

We grew up and knew that we were heading in different directions. I was going to UNR, University of Nevada at Reno. DJ was headed to Notre Dame. But I didn't worry about losing this friend. Our parents lived close, and at this point, Warren wasn't going to move again. So we had that anchor bringing us back to where we'd grown up together.

Besides, we were young adults. We both had drivers licenses and phones we didn't have to share with our families. When we wanted to see each other, we could make it happen on our terms. I was looking forward to meeting new people at college, and I wasn't worried about losing my old friends.

Then, with no warning, DJ was gone on April 2, 1996 at 3:30 p.m. A drunk driver hit him and killed him that summer, maybe a month before he was supposed to leave for school. All that potential, all that goodness and loyalty, all those years of comradeship were just gone in an instant.

For the last month I spent at home, I was lost. This was the first loss I had experienced of someone my age who was close to me, and it was beyond wrong—so far beyond that it was bewildering. How could you reconcile a loss like this? How could you make sense of it at all, let alone move beyond it?

You don't at first. You just feel like the world is dark and sinister. You have moments of pure, violent rage where you want to find the guy at fault and rip his head off. You have whole days of crippling lethargy where it feels like too much effort to brush your teeth. This storm of grief lasts as long as it lasts, and then it leaves you.

Your life moves on around you, and you have to move on with it.

That's what happened to me. And I hate to say that I learned a lesson from it, as if DJ died to teach me something. No—DJ died because someone was selfish and careless. But I did come off that season of grief a changed person.

I learned to pour as much of myself as I can into my friendships, because I know deep down in my bones that they cannot last. All of us are mortal. And I will never stand over another casket or hold another phone in my hand listening to someone cry and wondering how I left things.

Did I do enough to show my friend how much he

meant to me? Did I say the words I needed to say to honor the person who represents a vital part of my own life? If my friend thought of me at all before he passed, would the thought be a pleasant one?

I never want the answer to be no.

So once I invite you into my life, you are family. Period. If I have it in my power to do you a good turn, I will do it. If I feel like I need to tell you I appreciate you, I will say it. I will never leave anything for an opportune moment. Life doesn't guarantee you any of those. The other thing I did to deal with my anger and change my focus was to join the UNR boxing team.

In some of the following stories, I'm going to tell you about something I did for a friend here or there. You may feel like I'm bragging on myself about how much I gave away, like I'm some saint. You can forget that right now.

I'm telling you these stories for two reasons. First and most important is to set an example for you of how I live life with an open hand. I hope that you will read some of the stories I tell you and then think of someone around you with a need that you can meet. Maybe you are sitting on the resources that person needs thinking that they need to figure it out themselves or that you can't spare what they need and still be comfortable yourself. I'm here to be the voice in your head that says, "Give." You can make more money. You can't make more opportunities to use it for good.

Second, I'm telling you what I've done as a kind of confession. Look, I'm generous partly because of what

I've suffered through loss. I'm also generous in part because I'm ADHD and I have a soft heart. Again, I'm not perfect. I know that the flip side of my open hand is a lack of impulse control. Maybe you'll think that some of what I've done is a little over the top, and that's okay. I'm all right with my choices. If I have to work on impulse control, at least I don't have to work on selfishness. If I had to choose, I'd rather learn to close that open hand sometimes than pry the fingers loose!

So, this value of friends as the real deal, the ones who are there for you, some of the most important people in your life, is why I bring my friends into my business ventures. I see my friends for the quality people they are, and I know that my interests could be in no better hands. If you can't say the same for yourself, maybe look at who you're inviting into your life. For me, I'm a hundred percent all in on the people I value.

Don't let loss be what teaches you that lesson.

6 | **Fatherhood** *(Part 1)*

Around this middle school/high school time in my life, I began forming expectations of my adult self. They weren't conscious. Little Joey didn't have a twenty-year plan. Most of the time, Little Joey didn't have a twenty-minute plan.

But that didn't mean that the feelings and hopes brewing inside me weren't real and becoming permanent.

For instance, I felt the truth about what fatherhood should be before I could articulate it in words. And what I felt made itself known to me more by its absence than its presence. I understood what should be available to me as a child and was not.

I understood that the person who was biologically responsible for my appearance on the planet should have stuck around and helped me navigate my life. He should have been a constant source of love and guidance as well as a solid tie to my identity and my purpose.

And this had nothing to do with his relationship to my mom. Things hadn't worked out between the two of them—fine. So you break up the marriage. You can't break up with your kid. That is just not something you can do. You cannot cut yourself out of your kid's life without leaving a huge, messy, painful scar.

Also, knowing that another person is doing what you should be doing is no excuse, either. Warren Gilbert did his best by me. I'm grateful as an adult for his presence in my life. But no good he did for me could erase the profound loss and grief of the father-shaped hole in my soul.

I knew deep inside at a formative level that fatherhood was meant to be present, close, involved, caring, and giving unreservedly. There should be no limits to what you would do for your kid. There should be no doubt in a kid's mind that he or she was the most important person in your universe.

Each kid should feel that at a heart level.

As a lawyer now, I see the difference in kids who feel this kind of acceptance and support and those who do not. Some kids get in trouble once and move on. Those are the kids with involved parents—two involved parents. The kids who stay fucked up, those are the kids with at least one parent who dropped the ball. Sometimes both did, but invariably, at least one parent rejected that kid in favor of some crass self-absorption.

Here's another thing I understood about fatherhood, or about parenthood generally. I understood the direction the benefit was supposed to flow. I understood a parent to be like a stem holding the head of a flower to the sun and feeding it life from the earth. That was the parent. The flower did not exist to provide for the stem.

In some ways during my childhood, I felt that I was providing a kind of emotional support I should not have been required or pressured to give. In those ways, I acted as parent when I should have been receiving as a child. Consciously, I only experienced a desire to be good, to bring happiness or comfort to someone I deeply loved.

Subconsciously, I felt that the reserves of giving and caring that should have been held in trust for the next generation were being depleted daily. An emotional circuit in my heart was shorting out. You could practically smell the smoke and ozone coming off my soul. I understood from a very solid place inside me that I did not want to remain an exhausted well for the rest of my life. I needed time, a lot of it, and I couldn't say how much, to replenish those emotional reserves in my heart and soul.

Together, these two inner convictions led me to a conclusion that I never questioned until life forced me to reevaluate. Here is what I knew: I did not want to become a parent.

I revered the weight of responsibility so completely that I did not want to set myself up for failure. I knew that the life I had lived so far had not fit me to meet that responsibility with success.

It was like parenthood was a thousand-pound sword. The sword was beautiful and worth wielding. But I didn't have the arm strength to lift it. People could talk to me all day about how gorgeous that sword was and how rewarding it was to fight with it. All the talking in the world wouldn't help me pick the damn thing up and swing it.

I knew it was a lost cause. So why bother?

This conviction was so complete and solid that I made sure any romantic partners knew how serious I was about it. I wasn't wavering. I wasn't going to change my mind. I wanted to be fair to everybody, and being fair meant being completely honest about what I expected from my life.

If I was going to parent anybody, it was going to be the Little Joey inside me who was still hurting, still lonely, still lost.

7 | Service

I joined the Air National Guard in Nevada when I was fresh out of college. This was before 9/11. So I wasn't motivated by the heightened emotion, rampant public patriotism, and visceral desire for revenge that motivated a lot of recruits after the towers went down. I am really lucky for several reasons that things happened for me the way they did.

First, I enlisted in the Air National Guard partly because I had this vision on what it would take to run for political office one day. It was college, the military, law school, lobbying, and political office. I was fulfilling a requirement for the future I envisioned.

Second, I joined partly to pay for school. Lots of people before and after me have joined for that same reason. School now is insanely expensive, and unless you're a genius, a trust fund baby, or the kid of some lucky people who planned well, going to college means that you're on the road to permanent debt without an alternate plan. The military was my alternate plan.

Third, I admired the military. I could see that it had turned my quiet stepdad into a force of nature. I couldn't help but attribute his iron will and solid discipline to military influence. I thought I could do worse than let that training rub off on me.

Fourth, I liked the challenge. When I found boxing, it taught me that rigorous, consistent exercise was my friend. I knew that basic training and PT were going to provide external reasons, like boxing, for me to get strong and get rid of some excess energy. Cool.

So I ended up in the guard and discovered pretty quickly that I was not a good fit. Frankly, I didn't like following orders. I didn't like someone else deciding what I was going to do and not do. I didn't like being micromanaged. Being in a military environment didn't make me feel that I was becoming like my Dad. It made me feel like I was still living in his house, a ten-year-old kid who had to clean up after the dogs and horses because he said so.

Being in the military was a great experience for me, and I'm glad I did it. However, I don't like being praised as a veteran. Other guys took gunfire; I didn't. Other guys lost friends or their health or their peace of mind; I didn't. Let them get the high fives and the discounts. I don't want any of that.

What I do want is to support veterans in specific ways that I can from the position of life I've won. I am a good lawyer. So I can provide free legal services to veterans in need. I'm glad I can do that.

I'm also able to open and run dispensaries for medical marijuana. Because I own the businesses I do, veterans in pain and distress have access to a natural remedy without the disastrous side effects of opioids and benzodiazepines, like suicide ideation and depression. My business ventures mean that fewer veterans will take their lives. I think that's incredibly awesome.

This Country is a great country. The legal framework that brought it into existence is a work of genius. Our Constitution is the envy of the world. I love America, and I love the people that put everything on the line to defend her.

Veterans are like family to me. Anyone who has served or who has grown up in a military family like I did can tell you that instant connection and trust that you feel around people who serve. So although I'm not loud about my time as one of them, I'm proud to count them as an important part of my personal community.

8 | Relationships

When you're ripped from everything you know, you can start acting like an enhanced version of yourself—like you're a game avatar loading up on weapons and powers. All that extra pizzazz seems like good protection. And when you're an awkward kid just starting to notice that your body is turning on you after over a decade of dependable service AND you find yourself in a strange place around a bunch of strangers, you take every opportunity to exaggerate. At least that's what I did. I have a feeling I'm not alone.

I genuinely love Nevada now. I enjoy traveling with my work and for pleasure; I can name a lot of places I love to spend my time. (Hawaii comes to mind. Florida. California. What can I say? I'm a beach guy.)

But Nevada feels like home now in a way I could never have predicted when I arrived. You can't run for decades in the desert mountains, watching the sun rise and smelling the sage and creosote, and not develop a serious attachment.

You can't log all your adult milestones in one place, binding yourself there with ties of blood and treasure, without giving that place your heart.

Nevada is the place where I made my own family and

created my own success. I love Nevada for what it is and for everything it's given me. This place has molded me in a lot of ways into the person I am now.

But when I first got here? It just looked dead. I felt like somebody blindfolded me, spun me around, and stuck me in a Wile E. Coyote cartoon for a joke.

Seriously, I cannot communicate the depth of my hatred for Nevada at first sight. I begged night and day to go back home. I called my grandparents, especially my Poppy Aiello who helped raise me, and cried on the phone. I promised any number of good grades and clean rooms and anything else that came into my head if I could just go back.

One situation created some major trust issues. Mom and the Lieutenant Colonel worried about my grades, never spectacular, which took a nose dive after I arrived out west. They promised that if I got straight As, I could go back to Chicago.

You have never seen a more motivated kid. I studied hours every night. I went to every tutoring session the school offered. I did extra credit. And I got those grades up.

Then my parents changed their mind and said no, I had to stay where I was. I called Poppy Aiello heartbroken to beg him to come get me.

With all the love in the world, Poppy told me, "No, Joey, this is your family. You can't break up your family. You have to stay with them."

I understood that family first was a deeply rooted value for him. I loved him, and I understood how much he loved me. I even sensed that telling me no hurt him. But I still felt rejected and disappointed and angry. Having that last hope jerked away from me sure didn't make me love Nevada any more. It didn't make me feel at home with anyone around me.

The kids here made no sense to me. Back in Chicago, I'd had a place in the pecking order. I had guys to watch my back. Here, the kind of outdoorsy, sportsy guys who rose to the top of the food chain were a different breed.

They were Western kids. They listened to country music and drove pickup trucks. The desert was second nature to them. Their heads were full of John Wayne and Pecos Bill along with Kurt Cobain and Mike Meyers.

They had a view of themselves as real masters of the universe, owners of the land where they stood. They never seemed to question themselves or feel out of place. The shit they thought was funny puzzled me. And then it got personal.

They sure thought I was funny. They thought they had a right to do whatever they wanted to see just how funny I was. And I didn't like that one bit.

PART 2

HEALTH

"

It's not the size of the man, but the size of the heart that matters.

"

EVANDER HOLYFIELD

9 | Bullying

Before all the anti-bullying campaigns, middle and high school were something else. That series of John Hughes movies only scratched the surface of the eat-or-be-eaten ecosystem at school when I was young. Where I attended, the seniors thought they were gods. The juniors were demigods, and by the time you got all the way back to eighth grade, you had the social status and human rights of an amoeba under a microscope.

I didn't make things any easier on myself in that situation. I wasn't fat, but I wasn't athletic. I was what the older kids not-so-tactfully called "doughy." I also had a Chicago accent, a loud mouth, and a chip on my shoulder. I wasn't going to blend into any cowboy crowds.

So I became an easy means to an end for all the football heroes and basketball champs to prove their natural superiority. For the majority of my high school days, I was tripped, pushed, shoved into lockers, hit, teased, name-called, and generally belittled in a thousand different ways.

I did stand up for myself. My Dad had my back, too. I remember one time he stood up for me that made an impression.

This one kid was constantly picking on me. I say kid, but he was at least a head taller than me and thick for his age. Whenever I'd go through the door of the classroom, this kid would give me a shoulder, knock me to the side, and tease me. I got really upset about it. This was not one time; this was every day. I remember my Dad finding me crying one day and sitting down with me.

"What's up, Joey? It can't be that bad."

"This kid won't leave me alone. He's always there."

"Listen, Joey. This is the thing," Dad said. "You know your mom and I don't want you getting into fights. But if somebody pushes you around, you have every right to defend yourself. You don't need to take that," he said. "The next time he pushes you, deck him."

This was a Catholic high school, and they were pretty strict with the rules. They also preached love and peace, though that always seemed to apply to the victims, not the perpetrators. Sure enough, not a day or two after that heart-to-heart with Dad, the Neanderthal shoved me into the desks. So I stood up for myself, like Dad said. All that pent-up humiliation and resentment fired out through my fists, and I cleaned that bully's clock.

That day, Warren Gilbert got a phone call from the principal, and he and Mom had to go talk to him. Once they sat down with Brother Ignatius, he told them what happened.

Dad said, "Well, did Joey start the fight?"

Brother Ignatius said, "No, no, no, this kid pushed him, and Joey beat him up."

Dad sat back. "Then why are we talking about this? I don't understand why we're here. Joey defended himself; he didn't start the fight."

"Well, we don't let these kinds of things happen," Brother Ignatius explained. Which was seriously funny, because the staff had been letting these kind of things happen to me for quite a while, and I hadn't seen that mean kid's parents in here.

Dad told him, "You need to talk to the other kid about starting fights. What am I going to say to Joey? As far as I'm concerned, he didn't do anything wrong."

That felt good, standing up for myself and hearing how Dad stood up for me. But contrary to popular belief, standing up to one bully did not solve all my problems and stop anybody from picking on me. Much of high school was hellish.

Once the guys hauled me up by my ankles and tied me to the basketball goal in the gym just as the girls were arriving. They pantsed me. I had a choice between hiding my package and covering my ass. Guess what I picked?

Another time, the guys put me down into a cement-lined hole with a metal grate over it. Then they parked a van over the grate. Hilarious. I thought they'd come back in an hour, move the van, and pull me up. But they didn't. They forgot about me until that evening. They genuinely felt bad about that one, and their guilt bought me some time off and a kind of most-favored-freshman status.

Now all this special treatment taught me a lesson super early in life that I've used over and over again. That's the one right response to haters. You have three possible ways to go, but only one will save you.

First, you can rot inside. You can store up every bit of anger and resentment at all the bullshit you get handed, and you can index and catalog it. You can make yourself a real museum of bullshit that can sour your soul and make you fit for nothing but revenge and prison.

All these school shootings, you'll find that the perpetrators have curated bullshit museums where they spend all their time. Nothing good can reach them there because they're too busy pointing to the bullshit.

Second, you can curl up and die. You can let the abuse make you timid, someone who does whatever possible not to attract attention. You can adopt the belief that you deserve bad treatment. You can live in fear that the big people in your life are going to make you feel little. And they will.

I see these people all the time in my work now. So many domestic violence cases happen to good people who died inside enough that they think they deserve a bad partner. Over and over, the good people choose bad people because that's all they know.

Third, you can rise above the abuse. You can choose not to let what other people do to you stand as a true judgment of you. You can find it in yourself to laugh in the face of bullies and refuse to store their bullshit in your head.

This is what I did. The guys who never let up on me were seriously amazed that I never ratted them out to the administration. I'd show up to school with a black eye and say I tripped. They didn't know that I wasn't covering for them. I was being true to me.

Deep inside myself, I decided that I was too strong to need revenge. I was too solid to break down. I was too resilient to change to please others. I found that third way and rode it out of high school. I think it actually helped me later in life.

Although I was small for my age, I joined the Manogue football team and played my heart out, going up against players a head taller than me. This helped give me cred with the "big" guys.

If you think all the bullies exist only in high school, you're mistaken. Some of them out in the real world carry that senior jock mentality their whole lives, and you'll have to deal with them wherever you meet them. Lucky for me, I learned how.

10 | Boxing

People have asked me what happened to change me. What transformed me from "Doughy Joey" to a four-time Regional Champion, three-time National Champion and four-time All-American in boxing? What healed my relationship with the Lieutenant Colonel and let me call Warren Gilbert Dad again? What set me on the path to the great life I have now?

Boxing.

I know. It seems like a weird answer and like there should be more. Some people want me to have a deeper reason, some spiritual connection to a higher power or some intellectual aha moment. But I'm here to tell the truth, and the truth is that boxing changed my life. I was still dealing with the loss of my friend DJ, but boxing gave me a new focus and purpose.

After I left high school way, way behind, I went to college at the University of Nevada to study English Literature and Political Science with an emphasis on Foreign Affairs and Italian Studies. I had an idea of some things I wanted to do, despite the challenges that formal education presented me.

In college, I joined the Sigma Alpha Epsilon fraternity. It was full of guys kind of like the bigheads that ran my high school, but I was well-versed in dealing with them. At a party, the subject of boxing came up. I said I'd like to try it.

"Ha!" one frat bro laughed. "I'd like to see that! I dare you to join the team!"

Part of dealing with these guys is that you don't back down from a dare. So I didn't. I went straight to the boxing coach the next day and joined the team. I headed into a match within a matter of days with virtually no training, and I won.

How'd I do it? Easy. The coach taught me the rules. I could box to rack up points and win. The game of it appealed to me. From then on, I just had to get fit and strong to make it easier on me to score those points. It helped that my body had finally caught up to my actual age.

And I think that being ADHD actually helped me become a good boxer. I work well when I'm in an environment that would overstimulate anyone else. Even now, I work best when I'm moving around, walking on a treadmill or around my office, with the TV and the radio on.

So in a boxing match, where the crowd is screaming, the announcer is reporting, the cameras are flashing, your opponent is dancing, and the stimulation level is at a 20 on a scale of 1-10, I can relax and focus. The distractions work in my favor, giving my racing brain enough work to do so that the work of winning the match is slow and easy.

Or, at least, it's easy if you put in the work ahead of

time to get strong. All the hard parts of boxing happen outside the ring. And man, do I love the hard parts.

And here's one other thing boxing gave me. It gave me my Dad back.

I didn't tell my parents about my new obsession. I had fallen out of the habit of confiding personal things to them, and the changes boxing made in me felt so huge and permanent that I didn't know how to talk about them. I also didn't know how to bring up my immediate success without sounding like I had a big head. So I never mentioned it. Although, by my second fight, the cat was let out of the bag.

The newspapers didn't have any such reservations. I was part of the news, part of the college sports beat, and reporters described my fights. One reader of a Reno paper who knew the Lieutenant Colonel found my name in a write-up and showed it to the old man.

"This your kid, Gilbert?"

It sure as hell was, and the Lieutenant Colonel called me straight up to find out what was going on. He wanted to know all about the fight and all about how I was training and what had led me to want to box. We talked about all that, and suddenly, I found that I was just talking to him.

I didn't have to bring up yet again the ten years when he had misled me by omission about whose son I was. I didn't have to go through any of the hard questions or discussions I had assumed would have to come first before this kind of camaraderie between the two of us. I didn't have to open any doors to get to him. I saw now that, as far as he was concerned, the door had always been open. He had always cared about me, consistently, from day one. And all my hurt and confusion and resentment over his role in my life didn't change that role or how he felt about me.

There was just love. And there was some new pride. We could talk like two guys, and he could show some excitement about something that was becoming more and more important to me.

From that phone call onward, the Lieutenant Colonel never missed a match unless he absolutely had to. I could count on seeing him in the crowd, seeing his face. I could hear his voice goading me.

When I stepped into the ring, I found my number one fan—my Dad.

My Dad had boxed in high school and in the Marine Corps. After our discussions, and convinced that I was serious about my conviction to excel at boxing, he joined the coaching staff at the UNR Boxing Team and became the team physician and a ringside physician for USA Boxing. That partnership continued throughout my boxing career and really cemented "Team Gilbert."

11 | Weights

Here's what I learned from the first time I lifted weights. Lifting weights is hard. And it doesn't work overnight.

I remember walking away from the University of Nevada gym with rubber legs and arms wanting to curl up on the sidewalk and stay there. I never do anything part way, and I attacked my time at the gym like that was the last chance I'd have to workout there. Lucky for me I'm a good listener, and I trust people that know what they're talking about. I listened to my coach and worked out the way he said. I learned how to make the slow climb toward optimal fitness.

In fact, I learned that becoming and staying strong was going to take me the rest of my life. It was going to take every day for the rest of my life. I was going to spend some portion of every single day from the first time I stepped into a ring to the last day I draw breath running, lifting, and punching.

And that's okay, because that's what I want to do. Being strong is a priority for me. And I've received the message loud and clear that being strong is a daily decision.

I love taking pictures of empty gyms. You know why?

Those empty gyms are like a high five. They tell me, "Yeah, buddy! Way to show up!"

Listen, I've been running and lifting for long enough to know the patterns. I see full gyms in January after people make New Year's resolutions and in April right before swimsuit season. I know what that gets you— or what it doesn't get you.

Beyond not getting you results, it doesn't teach you the value of consistency. It doesn't give you the gift of the daily satisfaction of completing another step toward a goal. It doesn't give you the good energy of forward motion.

I don't have to panic and change my life in January or April. I wear what I want and do what I want when I want. I've earned the right to that kind of freedom.

When I lift, I'm climbing another step on the ladder that leads me to good health and peak ability. If I slack, I slide down a few steps. I don't want to do that. I want to wake up every day and grant myself that empty gym high five. I want to keep stepping up.

And I got hooked on that feeling pretty early on in my boxing days. I loved changing myself and seeing success consistently. I loved packing on muscle that would help me gain an edge in a fight. I could step into a college boxing ring with the confidence that the guy across from me might have skipped a day after a beer-and-pizza binge, but I hadn't. I'd put in the work. And now I'd get to add another big W to my record because I'd already put a lot of little w's in my column every time I woke up early or pushed for another rep or another 5 pounds.

Weights taught me the value of sacrifice. I'm there doing something hard when I could be somewhere else doing something easy. I'm giving up a warm bed and an extra hour of sleep. I'm giving up television or a night out with friends. There are real things I like doing, some things that are even good things, because I've decided on the priority that holds value for me.

And weights taught me the value of determination. Sacrifice is not fun and easy. It's worthwhile, and your thinking mind knows that it's worthwhile. But sometimes your emotions or your sore body argue with your mind that maybe you don't need to sacrifice today in particular. Maybe you can wait for tomorrow to get around to the sacrificing.

As much as weights train your body, they train your will and your mind. Without the mental edge to keep your emotions and physical resistance in check, you won't accomplish much. With that edge, you gain the freedom to win.

12 | **Nutrition**

I love good food. Man, there is nothing like a fat steak or a bowl of guacamole to put a smile on my face. Living where I do and traveling where I go, I can find world-class cooks putting out plates full of goodness right around the corner every night of the week.

I've trained myself to love the right food. It's a discipline you cultivate by exposure and practice. I've also trained myself to view food primarily as a means to an end. As I fighter, I had to know what would help me build muscle and shed fat, and I had to maintain the same kind of mental edge I needed in weight training to keep me feeding the machine of my body in the right way.

Pretty much all of us grow up eating the same way. You eat what Mom tells you to eat, plus as much junk as you can sneak or your Grandma can slip you. Some people have moms that skew healthier, while others have moms that skew more towards comfort food. You know what was in your refrigerator for snacks when you were growing up.

Because my Mom is Italian, we skewed more towards comfort food at our house. Not all that comfort food is bad—a lot of it has tons of vegetables and good meats, especially Italian comfort food. But I'll cop to a childhood starch habit that I came by honestly. And teenage Joey wasn't going to say no to normal American teenage fare: the hamburger-pizza-ice cream-French-fries kind.

People joke about the freshman fifteen, the extra weight that college freshmen usually put on when they leave home and take charge of their diets for the first time. When an eighteen-year-old-kid learns that he can basically eat fast food three meals a day and that that's the easiest option, he's going to travel down that road.

Boxing changed that mindset for me. At the same time I was learning about the consistent, daily work I was going to have to put in at the gym, I was learning about the way I needed to eat to maximize that work. I was understanding food as fuel. Food was yet another way I could game the system to gain an advantage.

The fact that I'm not actively boxing now doesn't really change anything. I like to keep myself in the kind of condition where I could pick up a fight and train to win without too much trouble. And that means eating consistently like a fighter eats.

To be able to keep up that kind of habit, I indulge in the best healthy foods I can find. I know that fresh, whole foods are a luxury for a lot of people. I work hard in part so that I can indulge in the luxury of providing the very best for my family and me. And I truly love that kind of food.

I get excited about nutritious smoothies and fresh-pressed juices. I love lean protein. I'm always up for trying food from around the world—the way the people in different countries have invented to use ingredients and spices amazes me. There is so much good that I truly enjoy that I don't miss the junk.

Do I have cake on my daughter's birthday? You bet. Do I still eat pasta at Mom's house? Are you kidding me? Of course I do. But my mind keeps track of what's a treat and pulls me back to what I need to eat for fuel when the celebration's over.

That's the whole deal for a lot of things. The will, the mind, has to be in charge. Everybody has a screaming two year old inside that can mess you up if you just try to keep it happy. But the adult part of you has to be the one making the decisions. That's just the way it has to be. It's a lot easier if you can love what's good, keep the adult and the kid inside happy. I do that.

13 | Cannabis

People who hear that I have a business interest in the Mynt Dispensary in downtown Reno might feel that it's not quite a reputable business for a successful lawyer like me. They hear the word marijuana, and they automatically make some assumptions about my values and lifestyle that are not justified. That's because marijuana has been given a bad reputation, on purpose, by government officials who, decades ago, wanted to associate it with minorities and thereby convince the largely prejudiced white public to avoid it and its users. They also wanted a pretext to criminalize those minorities, and marijuana was that pretext.

We've moved on since that time. No one of good character supports the kind of harmful stereotypes originally used in that publicity attack on cannabis. So why does marijuana keep such a bad reputation?

Chalk that one up to another publicity campaign, this one unintentional but just as harmful. People who choose to use marijuana recreationally have acquired a reputation as comical losers, intellectually slow deadbeats who get the munchies and provide comic relief for the rest of us. That reputation, though some deserve it, does not apply to the growing number of people who use cannabis properly, the way nature intended—as a legitimate medicine.

Listen—I'm into promoting the safe and responsible manufacture and sale of cannabis mainly for our veterans. Our veterans are coming home with PTSD and TBI (traumatic brain injury) in droves, and those regular folks - like you or me, who are living with PTSD—need this game-changing, life-saving medication. Cannabis allows for a much-improved quality of life without having to be on handfuls and handfuls of very harmful medications—THAT ARE NOT WORKING.

It's criminal that our veterans, whom we trusted to handle millions of dollars of equipment and arms and to represent us and defend us overseas, should be treated like children when they come home. Of course they should have the liberty to decide the course of their own medical treatment without suffering a punitive loss of benefits for refusing the zombie dope that is trapping so many of them in suicidal fogs and aimless lives. Cannabis is a wholesome, natural medicine, and our veterans have every right to choose it to relieve pain, sleeplessness, depression, and anxiety.

And why limit this medicine to combat troops? Shouldn't every American citizen have the right to choose the medicine they and their doctors agree is best for them? Why should ordinary Americans ravaged by cancer, Parkinson's, Alzheimer's, ALS, and a host of other chronic pain-inducing and neuromuscular diseases suffer needlessly when cannabis has been proven to treat all of them? Why should a politician have more to say about a citizen's medical care than his physician?

This incredible medicine treats so many illnesses and conditions. I personally have heard unbelievable stories of total life transformations for patients (and their caregivers) across the world.

For some, they simply experience less pain, For others, they can finally control the pain so that they can actually live a somewhat normal and productive life. For others still, cannabis means the difference between being able to get out of bed or not because of the degree of pain they are experiencing. It's the difference between walking or being in a wheelchair, between suffering hundreds of seizures a week or a few or none at all. Medicinal marijuana relieves and corrects dozens and dozens of ailments and diseases.

I believe that cannabis should be legal, accessible, and responsibly produced. So I invested with a group of others in Mynt Dispensary here in Reno. And I know firsthand what care a scientific, accurate production facility takes to create a safe, standard product. When you embark on this kind of an industry, you're employing experts in hydroponic agriculture, chemical processing, scientific tests and measures, and even culinary design and production—all under one roof.

I know that our products and others created by licensed labs have to meet rigorous health and safety standards in order to be allowed to operate. Our growth and processing facilities are scrupulously clean and orderly—more so than food processing factories accountable to the FDA. I see the process of refining cannabis from start to finish every step of the way, and I am convinced that we are offering the best medicine available to those who need it with our *Kynd* line of products.

Then our staff checks records for government compliance and carefully monitors who is allowed into the sales room. Nobody is wandering off the street buying product for the heck of it. No kids are getting confused and picking up cool candy bars that will send them for a mental ride. All of our products go from the hands of our staff to the hands of fully vetted patients in childproof packaging. We take responsibility for our products seriously.

We've even helped heal the neighborhood we chose as our production and sales facility. We bought a building in downtown Reno that had been abandoned for ten years. It was a blight on the neighborhood, inviting crime and suicide. Refitting and refurbishing that building raised the tone of that whole area of the city. We put in new sidewalks, streetlights, trees, and landscaping, not to mention building a neat outer wall and an attractive store front. Mynt brought safety, cleanliness, and order to our neighbors when we moved in.

Like many of my other ventures, I first got interested in the cannabis industry when I read a book on a plane. I saw the potential and got my staff and close advisors started on figuring it out. Learning the facts about cannabis and the requirements of the industry from growth to refinement to testing was a huge task. Luckily, I didn't have to work alone.

Some of my staff and friends and I got to work learning as much as we could. We flew up to Canada and toured ranches. I talked to chemists and toured laboratories. I made sure I understood all that was involved in getting those in need the medicine they required, safely and efficiently.

When I started talking about making a production and dispensary facility available in downtown Reno, everyone laughed at me. One lady from the planning commission actually told me, "No way are you putting a dispensary in downtown Reno."

I should have warned her that the most reliable way to ensure that I do something is to tell me I can't. From that day, I started looking for connections and opportunities to make it happen. Fortunately, as someone who works with a lot of influential business owners in town, I was able to make the necessary connections and convince some powerful people that my dream of helping veterans and patients in need would be good for the city.

The final area we need to discuss is the legal issue. Most of the states are decriminalizing cannabis for medical use, some for recreational use as well. My main concern is for veterans and patients in need to get what will help them. So I work and donate to support people in office who share my vision or to replace them with people who will share it.

I'm not out to cherry-pick candidates all over the

state and the nation. God knows I have enough other things to do. If we have sensible people representing us who will do right by the American people, and treat them like independent souls with working brains, fantastic. If not, we all need to be part of the effort to elect representatives who will vote with the will of the American people in our best interests.

Enough said.

I'm excited and honored to be a part of this process. The right way to support cannabis is by regulating it and controlling it—keeping it away from our children but providing access to those who need it and rely on its powerful medicinal properties. We've found the way to do that in Reno. I hope the trend spreads across the nation.

14 | Supplements

The diversity and abundance of our world floors me when I think about it. You're constantly hearing some study about the health benefits of one food or another. Items sitting on your grocery shelf help fight cancer, heart disease, diabetes, and asthma. It's incredible.

And then you think about the items that aren't sitting on your grocery shelf because they're not common to your area or they haven't been discovered yet. I mean, how many people in the fifties knew about acai berries? Goji berries? Chaga mushrooms? The natural world is an incredible resource that we have barely begun to explore and understand.

That's one reason why I use supplements and encourage others to use them. The people who are creating these products get ingredients from foods and plants that aren't common to people who eat the standard American diet. Even if you're eating better than the Standard American Diet—which is nicknamed SAD for a reason—you can fall into a rut.

Think about it. We're all creatures of habit, and we like things to be easy and familiar. Even if you're watching what you eat, you can fall into a rut. Chicken, brown rice, and broccoli are definitely healthy choices. But if you're meal prepping the same things over and over, to make your life easier during the work week, then you're getting just a narrow spectrum of the nutrients available.

We don't even know all the potential benefits of dietary diversity. You may be neglecting a wide spectrum of the vegetables, fruits, and nuts available because they don't appeal to you or you don't know much about them. But what if someone finds out years from now that jicama or watercress or purple potato can cure cancer or slow aging? Wouldn't it be better to know that you've been examining all the possibilities of staying healthy and active for as long as you live?

There's also the issue of food quality in this era of industrialized farming. When you really start looking at the food you eat, and calculating its nutritional value, you realize that we're working at a disadvantage today. A variety of factors are working against us as consumers to make the food we eat less valuable, in terms of vitamins and minerals, than it was in the past.

If you looked at a working farm a hundred years ago, you'd see a farmer rotating crops grown from heirloom seeds on land his family had worked for generations. He'd know what crops depleted the soil, how they depleted the soil, and which other crops or grasses would restore those nutrients. He'd take advantage of the natural cycle of animal labor. The animal - horse or donkey or ox - plowed the field and ate some of the produce of the field. The manure produced by the animal enriched the soil. It was a perfect cycle, and on a small scale it worked well to maintain the humans in charge of it.

That all changed when machines entered the picture. First of all, the machines were too expensive for most farmers to buy outright; so a lot of them mortgaged family land to buy the machines. Then, the machines didn't run on energy produced naturally by the land, the way an animal did. It cost cash money to run and repair that machine. Just to work in the new way forced expansion. You had to work more land in order to be able to work land that way.

And nobody had enough heirloom seeds to work that much new land. They started buying seed from farming corporations instead of saving the seed from their own crops. So the variety gradually disappeared. There's a reason most people eat red delicious apples, iceberg lettuce, and the standard watery, tasteless red tomato. That's what the corporation is selling.

Now don't get me wrong. The nutritional value may have lessened, but some choices are still healthier than others. I'm not saying, "Oh, the spinach isn't as packed with iron as it used to be, so you might as well reach for the Little Debbies."

I am saying that we should be intentional in upping the nutrients we're getting. And if we know we're apt to choose a lot of the same foods regularly, let's acknowledge that and reach for some supplements that can diversify the goodness our bodies get. I regularly try new supplements to experiment with what works better and improves my athletic performance or the way I feel. I'm a work in progress, and I love finding healthy new ways to enhance my abilities.

Remember: if you're going to maximize the output of your heart, mind, and soul, you've got to maximize the efficiency of the body carrying them around. Nobody is a brain in a jar. Take care of yourself.

15 | **Optimal Self**

Becoming a success in one area of my life challenged me to look at the rest of life. I was eager to apply the lessons I'd learned in boxing to my mind and soul and will. I wanted to become my optimal self.

What had I learned in boxing?

Discipline and willpower. I'd learned that I was strong, stubborn, and principled enough to tell myself no when presented with temptations like skipping gym and eating shit. I knew that becoming that kind of person, a disciplined person, was a valuable asset.

Constant motion. You don't stay still in the ring. To stand without the traditional bob and weave is to invite a lot of pain. This principle squared with who I was as a person and validated my need to stay active!

Fists up. You learn pretty quickly that if you don't keep your guard up, someone is going to knock you down or make you hurt. Keeping your fists up in other areas looks like preparing, doing due diligence. I do my best in every area to fulfill all legal requirements, and stay financially strong, so that I don't leave myself open to misfortune.

Fair play. To win, you don't resort to kicks, blows below the belt, striking your opponent when he's down, or just going ham on somebody like biting an ear part way off (here's looking at you, Mike Tyson.) You trust your skill and ability to win, and you don't take unfair, undue advantage. Having been the target of a lot of bullies, it was a good feeling to be part of a world where fighting fair was the norm.

Perpetual vigilance. You score points by hitting your opponent in specific target areas above the belt, like the head and chest. Your opponent has his guard in place, but constant motion or fatigue give you opportunities to get inside that guard and land a punch. Land enough of those, and you win. But you won't land a thing if you don't keep your eyes open and your wits sharp.

I knew that I could combine those winning strategies from boxing and use them to win at life. I could use them to become the best version of myself. So that's what I set out to do.

One strategy I used was becoming the most teachable person around. If I saw someone around who knew something I didn't know, I'd ask that person to teach me what he or she knew. I didn't care if I looked ignorant or if I made a pest of myself. I was hungry for knowledge and strategy, and I took it where I could find it.

I'm still like that today. If someone on my staff knows something I don't, whether that person is another lawyer or a paralegal or an assistant, I learn from that person. If someone on my staff has a good strategy to use in a case, I'll use that strategy. I don't care if someone else looks smart as long as I win. Henry Ford said that you don't have to be the smartest person in the room; you can hire that guy. Look where that philosophy got him. Being teachable is just plain smart.

So while I was on the hunt for how to become the best Joey Gilbert I could be, I came across someone who influenced the rest of my life: Tony Robbins. His charisma, his common sense, his evident compassion for others, his brilliance, and his optimism all appealed to me. I wanted to be like that guy, and I figured the best way would be to take all the advice I could get from him.

I listened to him on YouTube and bought his books. And as soon as I could afford to go, I started attending his live events. Over time, I took his courses—every single one I found, I bought. And what's more, I ate them up. I applied everything I learned. I didn't just hang the completion certificate on my wall—I took the lessons I learned and changed my life, a little at a time.

Discipline, motion, preparation, fairness, and vigilance—I used these lessons from boxing and applied the wisdom I learned from Tony Robbins about planning, optimism, and faith. These qualities guided my decisions moving forward. And I also relied on other mentors, other men who knew me, believed in me, and cared about what happened to me.

I was graduating college soon. I checked in with one mentor in particular to discuss my next steps.

16 | Mentors

As a young man, I found real direction and help through several different mentors. One of them, Tony Robbins, I only met later, after I had listened to his advice and implemented it for a while. I still look to him as an example and a guide. Another mentor had been closer to me for much longer: the Lieutenant Colonel.

I finished college with a real sense of satisfaction and excitement. Despite the grim predictions of the doctor who diagnosed me as ADHD at age nineteen (hey, better late than never), I had completed a course of study. Also, I had kicked plenty of butt in the boxing ring. Now, despite the relief and pride I felt in my diploma, I knew which area called me most intensely. I wanted to go pro as a boxer while my body was still young and able.

So I shared those plans with the old man, who had become my friend, my mentor, and my number one fan. But he didn't see my future the way I did.

"Joey, you're right about your potential in boxing. You could be big. But I think you're wrong about what comes afterward."

"What do you mean, Dad? I have a degree."

"What are you going to do with an English degree?

78

Teach?" I didn't mind when he chuckled at the idea. I wouldn't want to see me at the front of a classroom, either. If ever there was a teacher who was going to call recess more than half the class days, it was me. "And the PolySci classes aren't going to help you much, either. You've got to consolidate them into a career now."

"So what are you thinking?" I was skeptical. I could see that Marine Corps glint in his eye, and I prepared to shoot that path down sooner rather than later. Hadn't he learned anything watching me in the Air National Guard?

"Jerry Maguire," he reminded me. "If you want to do that work, you have to be a lawyer. Go to law school. What is it, three years? Pass the bar at the end, and then you can go professional with a real backup plan for when your knees or your back give out."

Jerry Maguire. I had talked about that show-me-the-money-go-getter for a while. And evidently, Dad had been listening. But while I had only the vaguest notion of how Jerry Maguire got to be Jerry Maguire, Dad knew.

That's a valuable role mentors can play for you if you'll trust them. The ones who take the time to get to know you and care about you can reflect your desires back to you in a clear and revealing way. Dad had seen a career path that appealed to me, and he nudged me down it. Two other mentors that helped me with this decision, and others, in my young adulthood were Sig Rogich, advertising genius and ambassador to Iceland, and Mills Lane, legendary boxer, referee, tele-

vision personality, and lawyer. Thank God the Lieutenant Colonel brought our family to Nevada, where I
met two such stellar human beings.

During my junior year of college I signed on to a
study abroad program in Torino, Italy, because of my
minor in Italian Studies. I had a great few months
traveling Europe and absorbing the atmosphere in Italy. That time helped explain my earliest memories in
the Italian neighborhoods of Chicago, and it helped
affirm some qualities about myself and my personality in a way that tied me to something larger than me.

When I got back, I felt refreshed and energized. I was
ready for a new challenge like law school. I enrolled
in Thomas Jefferson School of Law and headed down
to San Diego, but first spent a year in the Air Force to
mentally discipline myself in preparation for the challenge of a rigorous law school curriculum. The summer before entering law school, after completing basic
training, I began my professional boxing career and
also joined the Nevada National Air Guard Reserve.
Not the typical path for a law student... but typical for
me.

PART 3

AMBITION

"

No one starts out on top. You have to work your way up. Some mountains are higher than others, some roads steeper than the next. There are hardships and setbacks, but you can't let them stop you. Even on the steepest road, you must not turn back. You must keep going up. In order to reach the top of the mountain, you have to climb every rock.

"

MUHAMMAD ALI

17 | Law School

One great thing about law school was the friends I made. I still keep up with those guys. Another was meeting Cuba Gooding, Jr. and telling him about how Jerry Maguire had led me to the law. But the greatest thing about law school was making it through and out the other side. Man, passing the bar is still one of the hardest and best things I've ever done.

I cannot properly describe to anyone how difficult law school was for me. If college was hard, law school was almost impossible. Succeeding depended on memorizing a million details and applying them. Applying and reasoning was in my wheelhouse. Mentally organizing large subsets of data—not so much.

Knowing the challenge ahead of me, I brought to it the tools I had under my belt. Discipline, motion, preparation, fairness, and vigilance—these tried-and-true boxing principles came to my rescue yet again.

Take discipline. A lot of my making it through law school I owe to sheer willpower. I had to decide daily, sometimes hourly, that I could finish school and that I would not quit.

For instance, my classmates and I got through class to our first midterms in October. The midterms were

83

brutal, the kind of brutal that makes you question your life's purpose. I know this because a lot of people in my class called home for reassurance and encouragement after they got back a whole lot of red ink.

My classmates talked to me and each other about those conversations. Some people's parents said things like, "If your heart's not in it, then don't do it," or "I know you can do this if you keep trying." They basically got either permission to quit or a big confidence boost.

I called home, too. Dad briefly listened to my woes and fears and basically gave me a version of "Cancel your night." Marines don't really do emotional support duty. They tell you to nut up and get back in there. Honestly, sometimes that's what you need. "Nut up and get back in there" is Marine code for discipline and commitment.

Another boxing principle that saved my ass in law school was constant motion. I knew from college that I was going to do a whole lot better paying attention and assimilating fact if I could move my body while I did it. I needed the distraction of walking, standing, or bouncing for my brain to kick into learning gear.

So I stood in the library. I stood through lectures. When a professor objected, I exercised my budding court argument skills by presenting the necessity of constant motion for my success. My professors got to know that I would out-work any of my classmates. I just had to keep moving to do it.

Seriously, when I studied, I'd go to the beach or to

24-Hour Fitness and take headphones to listen to bar prep courses. I'd take books on the treadmill. I used the motion my body craved to get my mind into gear. I also liked the ambient distraction of waves and gulls or music and other people working out. Another study aid was my Dad. He would help me with my sample study tests and often scored higher than me, smartass!

Even today, I have to have a stimulating environment to be productive. I'll have on the radio and the television while I'm on the phone with someone and going over a document. I walk around my office constantly. I'm more effective the more I do at once. Knowing this about myself, I can orchestrate an environment of maximum stimulus to increase what I can do.

Back to another boxing principle, keeping my guard up—preparing for every possible line of attack—came in handy! I numbered my enemies: discouragement, boredom, difficulty, and physical pain after fights. (I fought every chance I could, all the way through college and law school into my career.) And I made a plan to fend off every single one. I knew my weaknesses, and I placed a safeguard against every one.

Fair play? You know it. No one succeeds as a lawyer who doesn't learn in law school. You have to go there for a reason. You have to be good at what you want to do. That old saying that cheaters never prosper is God's honest truth. In the long run, none of them do.

And constant vigilance? The whole story of my passing the bar (which took me three attempts) is a lesson in constant vigilance. I had to watch for every chance to achieve that goal.

First of all, I'm going to acknowledge the raw effort I put into that test the first time around. I spent eighteen hours a day studying in preparation. If you're counting, that means I left myself six hours to sleep, eat, dress, and exercise (because I wasn't slacking off that!).

I had the bar prep, the b exam, on cassettes in my Sony Walkman. It covered the eight most tested subjects on the bar. By this time, after law school, I had moved into a more public phase of my boxing career, and I was fighting regularly.

Once I was training with Jesse Brinkley while I had my Walkman on. He came over, took the headphones off me, and put the earpiece up to his head to find out what I was hearing. I don't know if he thought it was some top-secret ninja instructions or a super-hype metal jam or what. When he looked at me, I put my hands up.

"It's torts. I've got to study."

He wrinkled his nose in disgust. "You are one sick motherfucker. Who listens to this?"

Me, that's who. Fighting made space in my head to absorb some knowledge. I wasn't going to waste that!

But after all that effort, I failed by less than a point. I petitioned the state supreme court for a regrade because some of the answers on the bar were subjective. I thought that maybe an examiner with a soul could squeeze another point out somewhere. But no dice.

Because I had some notoriety, the story of my failing

the bar made the rounds. I looked down at my phone once and saw the 786 number that I knew meant the news was calling.

A reporter named Steve asked me about the bar. "I have your exam results here in front of me, and I see that you failed. Are you going to take it again?"

That question pissed me off. I could hear in his voice that he thought I was some dumb jock who had no place in law school, that maybe I'd gotten my bell rung one time too many, and I should give up. So I made sure to correct him.

"Yes, of course I'm taking it again."

"When can we expect to see that happen?"

"As soon as possible," I snapped. "I'm taking the bar again. And then I'll take it again if I need to. I'm taking the bar as many times as I need until I pass it!"

But I didn't follow through. I got distracted with my career and blew the deadline to sign up for the next exam. I let that constant vigilance slip, and it cost me a lot of effort and time to make up for that mistake. I was in trouble. So I reached out to one of my mentors, Sig Rogich.

"At this point, Joey, all you can do is petition the state supreme court again, like you did for the regrade. Petition them to let you take the bar again. I'll help you."

Sig got in contact with Michael Douglas, a justice of the state supreme court. Douglas was a friend of Sig's and a boxing fan. I will be forever grateful to him that he carried that petition to the other justices and waited while they signed it. Those two men went out of their way to give me my second chance.

But I failed again. Because I was late, I had to sign up to take it on the computer. I got thrown out of the computer sign in and had to redo it. I was so rattled with all of that and all the stress of just getting into the seat to take it, and all of the late night studying for this second attempt that I failed by more than one point.

The third time I took the bar, I signed up on time. But I didn't cram. In fact, I didn't study a bit. I remember getting up that morning and deciding to take a Valium to relax and calm my brain down. I walked in there calm, not caring if I passed.

Looking around me, I saw that the other people taking the test bore the marks of cramming. They had showed up in wrinkled clothes with coffee stains, obviously unshowered and unshaven, with bags under their bloodshot eyes. It was a sad and stinky place. I stood out in my shined shoes, cologne, and button-down shirt.

And lo and behold, the first questions were all things I knew from my former study sessions. They had all been in the prep I had listened to. I was feeling pretty good. Then I hit the five essay questions. I read them and panicked. I didn't know how to answer any of them. There was always a thorny question of ethics and professional responsibility included, and sure enough, I had a real doozy on the paper.

I got up and went to the bathroom. I couldn't sit still and think. I was trying to write at a table while other people were typing, driving me nuts. My head was spinning. I needed motion and focus, and taking a deep breath in my chair wasn't going to cut it.

I splashed my face with water at the sink, and then I started jumping up and down and champ talking myself in the mirror.

"Just like a fight, JG," I told myself. "You can train for twelve weeks on what you think the guy is going to do, and then you get into the ring and have to adapt. You just have to adapt. You can do this! Third time's the charm. Come on, baby! Come on, Joey boy! You got this!"

The door to the bathroom opened. The proctor, suspicious of my prolonged time in the facilities, had come to check up on me. Finding me without crib notes or other means of cheating, he escorted me back in. It was just me and the bar then.

I'm going to tell you now that I have no idea how I passed. I should have done worse this time because I hadn't spent the time studying. I'd gotten as much sleep as I ever do and eaten a good breakfast that morning. But somehow, I got through.

When the results came out, a friend of mine called. I was busy in the gym, getting on with my life, when I saw his number.

"Dave, what's up?" Dave worked in state government. I didn't know why he would be calling me right that minute.

"You passed, fuckface! You passed the bar!"

"You're kidding me!" I was so happy that I didn't know how to react.

"Don't tell me you didn't know! Am I the first person telling you?"

"Yeah, thanks for the heads up!"

Despite the weird way I found out, and the little time to celebrate in my new life, I felt a great deal of satisfaction that the lessons of boxing had come through for me. Because I had spent the time to become a good boxer, I could now be a good lawyer.

Also, this phone call meant that I had fulfilled my word to the Lieutenant Colonel. The old man had wanted me to prepare myself for life after boxing, and I had done what he asked. As a fully certified lawyer, I was ready for life outside the ring. Now I could devote all my attention to life inside it.

18 | Contending

The next phase of my story shows the amazing things that can happen when you give yourself permission to chase your dreams. I was fighting professionally after law school, appearing at casinos like Harrah's and Caesar's Palace Tahoe. Bigger things were on the horizon, though, and when opportunity crossed my path, I was ready for it.

I had just finished a fight (which I won) and was walking back through the casino with a group of friends when I saw Sylvester Stallone at dinner. Sylvester Stallone!

I had admired him for a long time. What guy my age didn't? The guy who played Rocky and Rambo? Come on! But I identified with him more the more I learned about him. For starters, he was Italian and a boxer. Also, he was an English lit major, just like me (we're both Edgar Allen Poe fans). And I saw in him the same kind of ceaseless ambition that I saw in myself.

I knew that for the next phase of my life, Sylvester Stallone was the perfect mentor.

He was going to be filming a new reality series with Mark Burnett for NBC, and I wanted in. So when I saw him, I was determined to get a face-to-face. My buddies egged me on, digging elbows in my ribs and saying, "I dare you, Champ!"

I left them behind, did a kind of spin move around Stallone's security, and introduced myself to the big man. I told him about my college record, my persistence passing law school, and my dreams for the future. I told him why I knew I could win *The Contender*, hands down.

Stallone listened to me. Not only did he listen to me, but he paid such close attention to what I said that he could repeat it almost word-for-word a few weeks later when I met with Jeffrey Katzenberg, Sugar Ray Leonard, and George Foreman during the casting call. They must have liked what Sly said, because after the casting process was over, I was a contestant.

From the beginning, I found the process of filming reality TV immensely interesting. I'm a people person who genuinely enjoys conversation, and so the constant social demands of being on camera at any given moment never bothered me. I appreciated the chance to get to know the other fighters in the house, and to this day, I count some of them among my friends.

Reality TV was a learning experience in another way, too. I soon got to see the difference between the real conversations and relationships I experienced and the story the producers decided to make of that raw material. There were real disappointments, like the moment when Tony Bonsante chose to fight Brent Cooper, the guy that the fighters on my team had designated for me. My anger and disgust at that moment were entirely real.

Something else that was entirely real was the fighting. We all took advantage of the training, which took place at a world-class facility with top-of-the-line coaches and mentors. So when we got into the ring together, we were inflicting serious harm.

Serious harm didn't mean serious grudges. We honestly did get along really well together. And no matter how the producers made it look, Jesse Brinkley and I had a good friendship. Even though he later handed me my lunch in a professional fight, I respect and like Jesse to this day.

We not only got along, but we took advantage of every opportunity to live the professional fighter life that Las Vegas and television afforded us. Fine restaurants, luxurious gifts, massages, connections—we had a whole lot of fun. I got a taste of the kind of luxury I could expect where the worlds of boxing and entertainment met, and I loved it.

I had high hopes for doing well on the show, too. Though I hadn't expected to fight Jimmy Lange, I found that I was up to the challenge. It was really meaningful to me that my mom, Dad, and sister came to cheer me on in that fight. I'd fought and done well without them in college and after, but there was something special about seeing my mom so proud of me and hearing my Dad's voice booming out encouragement. I'm grateful they supported me.

What made that moment even more special was the fact that Dad got deployed to Afghanistan when I went onto *The Contender* series. Dad and I were very close in college in part because of boxing. Because Dad was on the coaching staff, he'd travel with me to the meets. Dad had already been deployed once during the war with Iraq in 2003. Not six months later, he got sent to Afghanistan. When he left, I went onto *The Contender*.

All of us contestants were sequestered, which meant that we had no contact with anyone in our families at all once we started filming the series. We weren't even allowed to speak with anyone at home until a couple of days before our first fight. We had to go through our challenges and training, and once we had our first match set up, we were allowed to contact family. For that first six weeks, I had no idea how Dad was, and I knew he was deployed in combat. It affected me; it was on my mind. I did well in all the challenges, but I was worried about my Dad. Anyone could tell.

Now, Dad got back from Afghanistan on a Sunday, not that I knew anything about it. That following Thursday, I was allowed to call home because I was going to be fighting that Saturday. Of course, they filmed everything for the show. So I was on camera calling home.

When I called home, Dad answered the phone. I heard his voice, literally the last thing I expected, and I lost it. "Pops, is that you?"

He said, "Yeah, I got home Sunday."

I just started crying and talking at the same time, my mind buzzing with joy at knowing Dad was safe. "I was allowed to call because I'm fighting Saturday. It's so great you're back!" I said hi to Mom and talked to her for a bit, and then I hung up.

Ten minutes later, my family got another call, this time from Mark Burnett. He didn't want me to know this, but Mark Burnett asked my Dad, "Can you be in LA tomorrow? I want you to fly down. Joey is a totally different person now. After talking to you, his whole personality changed. He's so motivated, so engaged now, and I want to surprise him. So I'm flying you down and arranging for him to meet you at a dinner."

Jesse Brinkley had a house there because his wife and two kids were with him. So the show arranged to have me eat dinner at Jesse's house Friday night before my big fight on Saturday. I had no idea what Mark Burnett was planning. I just came walking in, and there was Warren Gilbert, bigger than life, in the living room with the cameras. I just went nuts. It meant so much to see him, especially when I had worried for so long that I might never see him again. That following night was the fight, and they asked Dad to be in uniform and to sit in the stands with Mom and my sisters, Gina and Anna, for the fight.

I had trained really hard for this fight. But the problem was that the week before, I'd injured my right hamstring in one of the challenges. I had a very, very powerful right hook, and I would launch off my right leg to deliver it. But I couldn't. I had no power in my right leg with that injury. So right when I needed it most, going up against the number three ranked middleweight in the world, Jimmy Lange, my right hook was weak.

Still, I was determined to do my best. Now these were five-round fights. In the first two rounds, Jimmy Lange just beat me up. Hands down, there was no question. He didn't knock me out or anything, but he was just landing blow after blow. I was on total defense, and I lost those two rounds.

After the second round, Stallone came up to Dad in the stands. He said, "You'd better go talk to your boy, because he lost those two rounds. If he doesn't win the next three rounds, he's going home. You'd better go talk to him."

So Dad got up and walked through the stands up to my corner. He knelt by me and said, "Joey, you know Jimmy beat you those two rounds."

"Yeah, I know, Pops. I just can't do anything with this right leg."

"Well, here's the thing. You know if you don't win the next three rounds, you're going home. It's only pain. You've just got to ignore it and give this all you got these next few rounds," Dad said.

I knew that what he said was true. I remembered all the training I'd had growing up about doing your duty and giving all you had. And I figured I had a little more determination and a little more pain capacity left in me. I beat the crap out of Jimmy Lange those next three rounds. I still to this day don't know how I was able to just fight through it, but I did. I knocked Jimmy down twice for two eight-counts.

The fifth round of that fight, there wasn't one person sitting down in the stands. Everyone was standing and just cheering, just going wild. And I won! It came down to the decision, and I won that fight. That's when I became the fan favorite on *The Contender* series.

Dad was such a favorite that Mark Burnett asked him to come again the following week for one of the challenges. We did a harness race, where the boxers had to go around the track pulling this harness towing Dad in the back. We were like the horse on a chariot.

One of the other fighters, Peter Manfredo, had made a comment to me earlier during another challenge, when the producers had given a truck away to the winner of that challenge, and Sergio Mora had won it. Peter said, "God, I wish I would have won that truck. My car's broken down; my wife's pregnant. I really need a vehicle so badly."

Lo and behold, the show was giving away another truck for the harness race challenge. The first three finishers in the first leg of it got to go against each other for the second leg, and the winner of that won the truck.

I had a lot of stamina, and Dad started coaching me when I was pulling him, "Save some of your energy. You only have to be in the top three to get into that second leg." So, I sort of paced us so we were in the top three. The three that were going into that final round were Peter Manfredo, Jesse Brinkley, and me.

But during the break in between the two heats, I took Dad aside and said, "Pops, Peter really needs that truck, and I really want Peter to win it."

"Are you sure, Joey?" Dad said.

"Yeah. He really needs it, and I want him to have it. How can we do it?"

Dad told me, "Well, you have to make sure that he's at least in second place, and then you'd have to let him pass you up or something."

"Okay, I can do that," I said. Jesse wasn't the best runner. He was strong, but he didn't have the stamina. Peter and I had more of the stamina.

"Here's what we'll do then," Dad said. "If you're ahead of Peter towards the end of that heat, rather than let him pass you up, just stop before the finish line and let him go by you. Everyone will know that you actually would have won that race, that he didn't actually beat you."

Trust Dad to be looking out for me, even if I was determined to let the prize go. In that second heat, I was in the lead, with Peter following, and then Jesse. We got to right before the finish line, and Dad said, "Okay, Joey, stop." Then I set the harness things down instead of crossing the finish line.

Sugar Ray Leonard runs out and says, "Joey, you have to go across to win! Joey! You're not across the finish line!"

I let Peter go by. Then I explained. That moment of non-victory was one of the things on that show that made me feel the best. A good guy got something he really needed, and I shared a special moment with my Dad. Win-win.

Not too long afterward, I fought Peter Manfredo, Jr.

Peter and I fought a tough fight. By the fifth round it was a toss-up. I really let loose in that last round and was clearly beating him. I had him up against the ropes, and with twenty-three seconds left in the fight he was about to hit the canvas.

All of a sudden, he launched forward and head-butted me so hard that he put a two-inch gash above my eye which bled so much that they had to stop the fight. At that point it went to the cards to decide the winner. Everyone knows that I had won the fight and that I would get the decision. However, that was not to be.

Sylvester Stallone went up to my Dad in the stands and said, "We have to give the fight to Peter because this is Hollywood and we need to finish filming the series within the next two weeks. Because of the cut, Joey wouldn't be able to fight for six weeks. We need a boxer who can fight next week, so we have to give the decision to Peter." So that is what they did, and the entire crowd was booing because they knew I had won that fight.

When we left the ring, my time on the show was done. Of course, I wanted to win for both the status and the million dollars. But I'm proud of the way I handled myself on the show and for how far I got.

When I was leaving, Sly told me I was the heart and soul of the show. That meant a lot to me. I'd come to respect him even more during our weeks of filming, and I knew that he would be an example and an inspiration to me for the rest of my life.

19 | Boxing Career

After my time on *The Contender* was over, I maintained my connection to Sly as a brand ambassador doing appearances for fans of the show and representing products that he endorsed, including In Stone, his line of nutritional supplements. I counted it a great honor to spend time with Stallone and do what I could to promote his interests. When we were on a private plane together, I saw him working out and complimented his consistency.

"How do you do it, Sly? How do you stay in such great shape?" I asked.

"There are those who talk the talk and those who walk the walk. I do whatever the fuck it takes and operate on a 24-hour clock, just get it done."

That's what the great man told me, and it's a lesson I took to heart. I strive every day to walk the walk and get shit done. If it's good enough for Sly, it's good enough for me.

Not only did I represent *In Stone,* but I also represented other brands as a spokesmodel. Over the course of my career, I was sponsored by Nike and Jordan brand, Dolce & Gabbana, Hugo Boss, and D2, among others. Acting as a spokesmodel meant a lot of travel and attending a lot of events. I was pretty much on call 24/7. But I wasn't just a pretty face. I was staying active in law, and I maintained a perpetual physical readiness to fight, which I could fine-tune with a camp over a few months when I had a match lined up. So with all of the opportunity and the constant work, I was busier than I had ever been. I loved every minute of it.

Being that busy, though, showed me a way to maximize my efficiency. And at first, it wasn't even my idea! My buddy Drew, who now acts as chief of staff for the firm, latched onto me when I was globe-trotting and convinced me that I needed an assistant.

Drew's dad, who was in the restaurant business, was a big sponsor of mine all the way back to college days. I liked going to Pinocchio's Bar and Grille for lunch a couple of times a week when I was in town. I'd sit at the bar and chat with JP or his son Drew, whoever happened to be working.

One day Drew said, "Hey, you should hire me."

"Hire you for what?" I laughed. "What would you do?"

Drew said, "I don't know." But I could tell he wasn't going to let it go, and he didn't. From then on, every time I saw him at the restaurant, he'd try again. "Hey, let me work for you. I don't know. I'll pick up your dry cleaning. I'll do whatever. I don't care. I just want to hang out; I want to work out with you; I want to do more cool stuff with you."

And finally one day, I gave in. "Sure," I offered. "I'll pay you a thousand bucks a month, and you'll basically just be my assistant."

He was in college at the time; so that was a good little chunk of change on top of working at his dad's restaurant. That's what it was at first, just running some errands. It quickly evolved from there because of all the fighting and travel and brand engagements.

Drew got to be my external hard drive. He'd travel with me to sponsorship meetings and engage with high-level executives. He'd remind me of my schedule and make sure I was ready for whatever I had to do. His work let a part of my brain relax and expand, occupying itself with creative possibilities instead of details and processes.

It was a 24/7 hustle. The phone rang all the time. We both carried two cell phones when that was cool to do. Business was good. Financially, a lot of money was coming in.

Incredibly, Drew was flying home to go to college at UNR for journalism and public relations. It took him five and a half years to graduate because we were so busy. I could have felt guilty about that if I didn't see daily how his work for me was benefiting him, too.

He was maturing quickly into a seasoned businessman. He took personal responsibility to equal the energy of everyone else in the room, and he picked up on small details quickly with no ego. When he first started with me, he had long, curly surfer hair that he sometimes pulled back in a ponytail or a bun. Without my saying a word, because it honestly didn't bother me, Drew decided that he'd look older and more professional with a haircut; so he got one. Boom. Done.

From this experience with Drew, I saw the value of a team. Since then, I've expanded the team around me to include several dozen highly valued associates who take my vision and my energy and translate it into practical steps. I get ten times more done with them than I could do alone.

Fighting was one of the best things I've ever done. I can't describe the positive energy of that lifestyle. I was devoting my vast capacity for action to staying in peak athletic condition and honing my craft as a sportsman. Ridiculously gifted people poured their skill and their resources into perfecting my performance, for which I remain humbled and grateful.

Not so humbled that I wasn't kicking ass regularly, though. Out of 24 fights, I ended up with a record of 20 wins. I'm proud of my record and my achievements as a professional boxer. I got to perform at the height of my skill and power for thousands of people at some world-class venues like Harrah's, the Hilton in Reno, Caesar's Tahoe, the Eldorado, and the Grand Sierra. I faced some fierce challengers like Peter Manfredo, Jr., Juan Astorga, Jesse Brinkley, Keith Sims, and Kassim Ouma. Those memories will stay with me forever.

The only drawback, when I was young and single and kidless, was reckoning who I had to be inside the ring with who I was outside it. I'm a lovable guy. Growing up the class clown, a born extrovert if there ever was one, I used to hug and kiss everyone when I walked into a room. I had a happy, positive energy that made people smile.

But as a fighter, you have to be confident and aloof. When you step inside those ropes, you had better know that you're the fucking toughest guy in the room, because when times get tough, it's just you in the ring. You kill or you lose.

It's very true that you don't play boxing. Unlike other sports, boxing requires an edge of violence and an ultimate commitment to victory. That seriousness of purpose makes it an apt metaphor for life. It's only over when you quit or can't get up.

Boxing professionally made me more prepared for life than any other pursuit I've undertaken. Learning that discipline and commitment gave me the training and background for success in every other endeavor. It taught me not to give up or take no for an answer. It taught me to recognize the goals worth pursuing to the end.

Eventually, I found one goal worth surrendering this career for. And it's one that takes first priority to this day.

20 | **Haters**

One thing you can do that is guaranteed to piss people off is to take money out of their pockets. Another thing you can do is tell someone with some power that you want to go your own way. Do both things, and you're screwed.

I speak from personal experience.

Las Vegas is a fighter town. People come to Sin City to sin in all different kinds of ways—ways they wouldn't try back home. That's why you've heard everyone say, "What happens in Vegas stays in Vegas." It wouldn't have to stay here if you could bring it home.

Las Vegas is the place to find showgirls and strippers, magic shows and puppeteers, roulette wheels and blackjack tables. It's the place a tough guy can go for a Celine Dion concert and cry his eyes out without anyone thinking twice. It's the place a meek Sunday school teacher can gamble her Christmas bonus away, or maybe win ten times that if she's lucky, and never have a PTA chairman look sideways at her. You can indulge your impulses and fantasies here with little risk and no judgment.

For some people, boxing feels like that. It's cathartic

in a way they can't explain to see two big guys punching the shit out of each other, wiping away blood and sweat in between rounds, and maybe one of them taking a nap on the mat. People don't see that every day. It seems dangerous and exciting to watch and participate vicariously in raw violence that way in person.

And all of the people looking for that adrenaline rush pay a lot of money to the people that organize these fights. I'm talking a lot of money. Promoters get paid. A lot of times, they're doing a hell of a lot better than the fighters.

I had kind of known this truth all along. Remember Jerry Maguire? My reason for going to law school? Yeah, he was an agent, and that movie showed how, when there was a pile of money on a table, athletes were the last ones in line to get paid. There's a reason Cuba Gooding, Jr. had to yell, "Show me the money!" It's because someone else had it first. And more of it.

I was coming to box as a professional in Las Vegas from a very different position than a lot of other boxers. Usually a promoter had to engage in marketing the fighters they found. They had to make people excited about watching what their clients could do. They had to create some name recognition and a public face. They needed to create a reputation that other fighters would want to challenge.

The kind of Muhammad Ali trash talk that all fighters trade in doesn't work if you hear the insult and have to ask, "Who's he talking about?"

But I didn't need that kind of representation. I'd been

featured on national network television. I brought built-in name recognition with me. People wanted to know the rest of the story, how I would do after television.

So I honestly didn't see why I should give a big part of that pile of money on the table to some guy when I'd done all his work for him. It made no sense. I could pick up a phone and schedule fights with other promoters. I'd just start a company. Did I need legal paperwork or a license to become a promoter? Well, wasn't it lucky for me that I had a law degree so that I could do that myself, too!

I started Joey Gilbert Promotions and began setting up my own fights. That's when I found out that the fighting establishment didn't like what I was doing. It set a bad precedent for a fighter to represent himself. What if all the fighters started pulling a Joey and arranging their own fights? What if all that sweet, sweet cash went away for good to the guys who were actually spilling their blood to earn it?

Well, that couldn't happen!

All that angst centered on the Nevada Athletic Commission. And the head of the NAC, Keith Kizer, was hearing plenty from the ring of promoters that gave his commission something to do, a reason to exist. I'm convinced that what happened next was a ploy to smack me back down in my place.

There is no other explanation.

21 | Failure

I have, at different times in my youth, experimented with recreational drugs from shrooms to marijuana to cocaine. While I was tempted to try these, I wasn't tempted to try others. While I'm blessed that—despite how hardheaded I was as a young man—I never got caught up in that lifestyle, I'm going to share with you a drug accusation that wasn't true about me yet affected me and my future all the same.

I fought Charles Howe at the Grand Sierra Resort on September 21, 2007. Before that fight, I completed a pre-fight questionnaire. On it I disclosed Adderall and Valium. I wasn't taking any other prescriptions. I definitely wasn't taking anything illegal. I cared too much about my body and my career to mess with anything like that.

That fight ended with a first-round knockout. I was thrilled with the victory. I gave a sample for a standard urinalysis after the fight and went home. The next Tuesday, my world blew up.

The commission notified me that a whole laundry list of drugs showed up in my urine. They were pursuing consequences. But while they were pursuing consequences—not investigating the accuracy of the claim at all—they decided to smear me in the media.

Overnight, my life went to hell. The name recognition that had been my meal ticket for years suddenly became an explosive pink slip. The public wanted me fired. And they let me know in a lot of ways.

I got internet trolled big time. I couldn't go out in public. I couldn't even get gas around the corner from my house without some goon yelling insults at me. As for going to a gym? Forget it. Toxic city.

And the thing was, I had not done one single thing wrong—nothing to deserve the kind of public shaming that was being heaped on me. I had not cheated. I had not taken any unfair advantage—not that anyone in charge was asking. As has been shown by the kind of changes they made after my case, the NAC conducted haphazard, non-standard testing of athletes and participated in libelous publicity. If I had fought that same fight with the exact same conditions today, I would not have endured the months of hell the commission sentenced me to without a fair trial.

Here's what any boxing commission would have needed to know on the kind of questionnaires that are standard today.

First of all, remember that I'm legitimately ADD & ADHD. Substances don't work with my blood chemistry the way they do in someone who's not ADHD. I have a prescription for Adderall that slows me down and helps me focus, just like half the kids in this country. Someone who doesn't have my blood chemistry takes Adderall to hyper-focus and stay awake. That's not why I take it.

Also, there is no shame in taking a focusing medication that a doctor prescribed me. There's no shame in having the brain and physical makeup I do. Despite aspersions cast in the media, having ADHD and dealing with it in a medically acceptable and responsible way should in no way disqualify me from participating in organized sports or anything else I choose to pursue.

Second, I was coming back from Operation Iraqi Freedom. As the son of a Marine Lieutenant Colonel, I couldn't think of anything more worthwhile to do with this celebrity the commission resented so much than go meet the troops and give them a moment to think about something besides being uncomfortable and getting shot at. So I went with the USO on one of those huge C-17 airplanes.

I wouldn't change a thing about that trip except for the plane. I had to sleep on one of those cargo nets, and between the noise and the lights and the motion, that wasn't happening. So I took a Valium to help me sleep. I didn't take Valium regularly, but I knew that one dose I'd taken on the plane would stay in my system for about a month. So I disclosed it.

I did not disclose the herbal supplements I took. There was no space on the form that asked about herbal supplements, and nothing I took was not available to anyone walking into a GNC store or browsing sports supply online. This was standard stuff—antioxidants, greens, acai berry powder, and kelp—that kind of thing.

As an athlete with some recognition in the public eye, I regularly received samples from supplement companies who wanted my endorsement, and I tried stuff out for them. Nothing I took listed any illegal substance on the label. I had no reason to suspect that any natural product I took for my health would jeopardize my health or my standing in any way.

You want to know how nuts I was about keeping my blood and body clean? I had to have nose surgery, and I didn't take the prescribed Percocet for pain. I was the risk management officer at my fraternity house, making sure that the guys stayed above board and legal. No one would have risked the fraternity charter on me if I wasn't going to do the job. Everyone in my life knew where I stood on illegal substances.

Besides, I'd been fighting in the public eye for a good nine years by that time. Since college, I'd never gone up a weight class. Anyone who knows anything about the kind of booster shit the NAC was claiming I used knows that it packs on muscle and weight. There is no way I could have stayed in my weight class if I was abusing steroids.

For sixteen months I fought that ruling. That's sixteen months that I couldn't fight, couldn't earn a dime with my fists. Sixteen months having my name dragged through the mud. Sixteen months fighting depression and anger. And the only defense I could mount besides telling the truth was trying to reverse-engineer exactly how the NAC had screwed up and explain it to them.

I got my reserve sample back from the lab and sued the lab—Quest Diagnostics. The only thing I can guess happened is that either somebody with a grudge knowingly tampered with my sample or that there was some kind of lab error. No matter what happened on their end, the NAC handled the entire situation irresponsibly and harmfully in the public eye.

I was perceived as an outsider, some big-shot TV celebrity who wouldn't play by everyone else's rules. The head of the boxing commission thought that I didn't deserve to have the kind of fame I had. There was no way he was going to be impartial about anything to do with me.

That dislike of me that circulated among the people in charge spawned this whole drug-testing fiasco. Combined with the haphazard testing protocols of the boxing commission at the time and the media circus that the commission encouraged, that dislike got me into a whole lot of trouble. And it was trouble that pounded several valuable, uncomfortable, permanent life lessons into me.

First, I've learned never to underestimate haters. I always assume that someone who dislikes me and wants to show me up will hit below the belt and get away with it. So I prepare for that possibility now.

Second, I've learned that I can stand pretty much anything. Public hate that felt like it would kill me eventually went away. Professional setbacks that felt permanent went away. Surviving to fight another day was my job during the dark days, and that's what I did.

Third, I've learned that the people who matter will stand by you, and the people who don't stand by you don't matter. I count among my nearest friends the people who stayed true to me despite the lies that were circulating everywhere. They believed me, and they believed in my ability to fight my way back. I'll always be grateful to them for that support.

One of those people was my Dad. He was in Iraq on another combat deployment when this was going on. I was able to contact him, and we spoke about how I should proceed. He was well-versed in the ins-and-outs of drug testing, and he had total faith in what I was saying was true. He encouraged me to fight it and use a trusted lab to get retested and retest the original urine sample. That is exactly what I did, and the result came back negative for illegal substances.

You know, that time in my life was a lot like high school, but worse. Kizer and the NAC acted just like the senior jocks that thought it was funny to pants me or leave me in a hole in the ground. But I look around now, and those jocks are nowhere to be seen. I am. I look around now, and Kizer is nowhere to be seen. I am. Truth lasts. Truth wins.

Even if it takes a hell of a lot of time and pain to prove.

22 | Work Ethic

Oscar De La Hoya is a boxing legend with a statue in the Staples Center. Ever since he dominated the 1992 Olympics, he's been at the top of the sport, setting records and taking wins. He even preceded me in the self-promotion game, creating Golden Boy Promotions in 2002 to arrange his own fights, among other things. I respect the man.

De La Hoya has a house in Big Bear that's outfitted like you would want a fighter's house to be outfitted: weights, sauna, equipment, training ring. And it's out in the wilderness where a person can go run without meeting anything more inquisitive than a coyote for miles and miles.

That house is where I went in January 2008.

For two months, I had stayed inside my house and didn't leave. I basically stayed in bed and took Xanax. My career was gone, and I thought that I might be disbarred, too—all because someone had either lied about me or made a disastrous mistake. I was royally fucked, and there was nothing I could do about it.

Why train? Why get up? Why answer the phone? There was no point to anything at all. I had lost everything that meant anything to me.

So the rare times I did go out, I was pale and sick-looking. Circles ringed my eyes. I lost weight. My appearance stoked the lies and made everything worse.

I was going out to meet with other lawyers about my case. I worked every angle to prove my innocence, and I spent over sixty thousand dollars on attorney fees and court fees. I passed a polygraph and was told it wasn't enough to prove my case. My obsession wasn't good for me, because a lot of what was happening was out of my hands. It was time to let the people who were outside the mess work on untangling it.

I was friends with a bunch of UFC fighters—real stand-up guys who knew me and knew not to take the bullshit rumors about me at face value. One of them, Diego Sanchez, was staying at De La Hoya's Big Bear house and training with other fighters there: the Diez brothers, the Ortiz brothers, Theodore T. Diego called me on his birthday at the end of December and invited me to come train.

His invitation struck a chord with me. I knew the healing effects of hard physical training. And as a people person, I needed good company to heal mentally and emotionally. The self-imposed isolation was not helping me.

My girl Molly encouraged me to go. So I went. It was the only lifeline I saw, and I grabbed it.

Immediately, being in Southern California helped me. I was away from the worst of the publicity. And I had happy memories of this part of the country, where I'd gone to law school. I felt like I could breathe better as soon as I arrived.

One event set me on a good path. I was watching Richie and Tito Ortiz sparring, and Diego invited me up to the ring with Tito. "Can you give me a southpaw look?"

I hadn't trained for two months and didn't know how I'd do in the ring again. But I was game to try. We started sizing each other up, and I saw an opening. I hit Tito so hard he wobbled. From that moment, we were lifelong brothers. Man, that felt good.

Now these UFC guys were beasts—strong and tough. But they didn't have formal boxing training, which is not all about just scoring the points that win you a match. I knew how to go for a strategic advantage. They didn't know how to turn their hips. One hit in the floating rib, and they'd go down. I used to hurt my hands hitting them. I almost switched to UFC because I was so good at fighting them.

That fight sparked a resolution in me. I wanted my belts back. I wanted to come back badder than ever, test clean, and put everyone who'd ever said shit about me to shame when I won every match I entered.

So I trained harder than I ever had in my life. I'd do altitude runs with a weight vest. I lifted like a madman. I'd run in the dark with a headlamp on, even in three feet of snow. I worked every day to beat the leader on Peloton.

I fought all the time. I learned whatever the other guys could teach me: Jiu Jitsu, Muay Thai, kickboxing. I wanted to know every trick in every book.

I started training in San Diego gyms. People would see me, Google me, and come up to ask me about the steroids. I had to take a lot of shit and answer a lot of questions. But eventually these guys saw how hard I was training. They knew I didn't have a fight coming up; I was working insanely hard for the principle of the thing, without knowing if I'd ever have a chance again to make the hard work pay off.

That daily commitment won me respect. I made relationships in Big Bear and San Diego that saved me. Regaining my health and fighting fitness made up a huge part of the healing process that brought me back from the dark place that had imprisoned me in the fall.

When people asked me how I could come back after what happened, I give all the credit to my work ethic (thanks, Dad). I never stopped training. I always knew I was coming back.

And here I am.

23 | Consistency

I was ready to come back. I had fought in court, come back stronger physically, and healed mentally and emotionally. I was healthier in every way coming back than I had been when I left.

But the commission kept making me wait. They wanted me to cut a deal, admit that banned substances were in my body. They were in total CYA mode, because they had messed up royally by smearing me in the media before all the facts were in. And as much as I hated to give them an inch of ground, I had to face the reality of the situation.

They could decide whether I would box in Nevada ever again. They were going to bar me permanently unless I helped them save face. So I admitted to having a previously undisclosed substance in my blood as a matter of expediency. I knew that I had to do something to get back into the ring, and I did it.

It didn't matter. I knew the truth. I'm convinced they did, too.

Then I arranged a fight with Jesse Brinkley, my old friend and nemesis from *The Contender*, for Valentine's Day 2009. I went back to Big Bear and doubled down on training with Richie Ortiz, Diego Sanchez, and

Matt Pendola.

Pendola is a premier strength and conditioning coach. I still work with him today on maintaining peak fitness alongside elite athletes. He's one of the reasons I know I could still pick up another fight. When I was preparing for this February matchup with Brinkley, an event we billed as the Civil War, Pendola was invaluable to me.

In preparing for this fight, I distilled three principles for daily success. They'd been forming in my mind for the past sixteen months, but now I acknowledged them consciously and committed to practicing them routinely. I still do.

Here they are:

Step 1 to Daily Success is Forward Motion: Get Up and Get Moving - DON'T casually stroll into the day. Hit the floor, and hit the day with intensity and focus. Meet the challenges of the day with purpose and conviction.

I usually wake up at 4:30am and run 6-12 miles before preparing for my court cases for the day. I like to feel that I have completed a full day of work before 8am. If you do not move, you will be passed by people who do. It does not take much for your body to react to new challenges and obstacles. Push yourself. Always remember, too, that you cannot outwork a bad diet.

A champion's heart is made of gold, and that means you don't quit. You fight on. I have stayed in the trenches to fight for Nevada, fight for the community, and most importantly, fight for the great principles of liberty and justice that built this nation.

Step 2 to Daily Success is Touching Base: Do One Thing to Better Yourself Every Day. Whether it's a morning workout, morning meditation, yoga, Pilates, stretching, or walking, just get it done. We all know what we need to do to be better. YOU JUST HAVE TO EXECUTE.

From there, take time to have a conversation filled with optimism and love with a family member, colleague, a significant other, or friend. Once you better your health and better your relationships daily, everything else begins to take shape. JUST DO IT!

Anyone can train to be a gladiator. What marks you out is having the mindset of a champion.

Step 3 to Daily Success is Intentional Intensity: Push the Pace, Stay in the Pocket, and Keep Throwing Punches. Tackle your objectives with fierceness and conviction. We are all capable of fighting harder and accomplishing more throughout the day. Whatever is on your list, whatever your objectives are, push pass those HARD & FAST.

When you stay motivated and avoid distractions, you give yourself more time for your mental fortitude, and the day opens up to spend with your loved ones. Truly keep fighting and looking for more ways to better yourself and create that edge. My man David Goggins says, "Stay hard."

But I want to say: stay in it —push the pace —stay in the pocket —keep throwing punches —keep moving forward. It truly doesn't matter what time of day it is or where you are. Stay focused, and keep getting some. Get shit done. It doesn't matter how hard you get hit or if you get knocked down; it matters that you get up and fight on.

These three daily steps for success work for me. The key is that they are daily steps. You do them EVERY DAY. NO SKIPPING. I guarantee you that if you spend the next 30 days implementing these steps for yourself, YOU WILL BE SUCCESSFUL in your personal life, in your business, and with your relationships.

Forward Motion: Get Up and Get Moving

Touching Base: Do One Thing to Better Yourself Every Day

Intentional Intensity: Push the Pace, Stay in the Pocket, and Keep Throwing Punches.

Tackle your objectives with fierceness and conviction. Please reach out with any success stories. I would love to talk to you!

And now it's time to tell you a hard truth that I don't want to discourage you. It sure didn't discourage me! Sometimes you do give it everything you have and more, and you don't win.

That sucks. It shouldn't stop you.

On Valentine's Day of 2009, I fought with everything I had. Literally. I lost 11 pounds of blood and water in that fight. You talk about leaving it all on the mat; that's what I did. But I lost. Instead of the Civil War, that fight became known as the Valentine's Day Massacre.

In round five of that fight, I bounced off the ropes, and as I was moving forward Jesse caught me with a straight right that literally crushed my nose. It bled profusely, but my cutman, Carlos, was able to stop the bleeding. Everyone in the stadium gasped and figured the fight was over. When I went to my corner after that round, I told my Dad to please not let them stop the fight. He asked me if I was sure about that, and I answered yes.

He agreed to honor my wishes, and as long as Carlos could control the bleeding, the referee would not stop the fight. Three times over the next seven rounds, my nose was bleeding so heavily that the ring physician went to my corner and told my Dad that he should stop the fight. My Dad told him, "Do Not Stop the Fight," and so he didn't. Much to everyone's amazement (everyone but my Dad), I went the whole remaining seven rounds and lost the fight on a split decision.

After the fight, my Dad went with me to the hospital to get my nose x-rayed, which confirmed that it was fractured in multiple places. I was upset that I allowed myself to get tagged the way I did, which led to my losing the fight due to the constant blood that I was swallowing, not being able to breathe properly, and the severe pain in my face.

This is what my Dad said. "You being able to persevere for seven rounds after getting your nose shattered was one of the most amazing displays of sheer

will, guts, and determination that I have ever seen."
He reminded me that I lost the fight in a split decision because, despite my injuries, I fought back and almost knocked Jesse out twice with vicious rights of my own. Jesse actually spent the night in the hospital as a result of the blows I landed...some consolation, but a loss is a loss.

So I had a choice. Was I going to continue my boxing career in the same way I had, no matter what it cost me, or was I going to direct my energy and focus and determination to win into another area?

24 | **Fatherhood** *(Part 2)*

Before I talk about this part of fatherhood, I have to talk about my daughter's mother. That's a difficult conversation, because we're not together now. So this story is a story with different perspectives and different expectations and disappointments. My intention is to be as honest and as kind as I can be, knowing that three people's hearts will be directly affected by whatever I say and knowing that my daughter will read these words sooner or later.

So here goes.

Molly and I both attended the University of Nevada at Reno, but not at the same time. By the time she started as a freshman, I was on to law school and *The Contender*. I'd gone back to UNR to host and comment on a boxing event for college-level fighters from across the country.

She came with her dad, who was a fan of TV Joey. He wanted to meet me in person, and he brought Molly over with him. I could see right away, besides the fact that she was absolutely beautiful, that she was very close with her dad. I soon found out that they worked in real estate together. So not only was Molly beautiful, she was also smart, driven, loyal, and friendly. Of course I wanted to get to know her better.

We started dating, and pretty soon after that, I had a serious talk with her. She was very open with the fact that she wanted a family, with marriage, kids, a dog, and a white picket fence. I told her as plainly as I could that I was not that guy.

By that time, another factor had added to the original conviction that I was not going to settle down and be anyone's father. I had embraced the whole killer mindset of professional boxing.

If you are going to win belts and titles, you have to be the lion stalking prey. You have to keep some sharp claws honed. You can't be too tame and still find that fierceness inside you that looks at an opponent and says, "I'm going to tear this sumbitch apart."

Serious romantic relationships were not going to help me keep my edge. I love women. I love finding chemistry with a woman, getting to know her, sharing romance with her, and sharing intimacy. But I felt that I needed to keep those relationships both temporary and light so that I was not investing any energy I couldn't afford to lose.

Besides, if we're being 100% honest here, I just couldn't imagine being with one person and only one person for the rest of my life. It seemed boring and confining. I didn't see the attraction in a permanent, monogamous relationship. The pursuit, the interest, the excitement of initial attraction, all of that would disappear with permanence. That was not what I wanted for my life.

I explained that reality to Molly very early on in our relationship. I told her what I could offer her and what I couldn't. She was still interested in being part of my life. But from the beginning, I thought that she would eventually get tired of me and find someone who would give her what she really wanted: the white picket fence in the suburbs.

We had a clear understanding. When I was in town and we were together, she was my number one girl. When we were away from each other, we were both free to see whoever we chose. With that understanding between us, we enjoyed the best span of our time together.

Molly became my best friend, the person I trusted and consulted and looked forward to seeing. I brought her down to San Diego to law school to spend time with me. I wanted her around. Beyond our amazing chemistry, we had an amazing friendship. I admired her ambition the same way she admired mine.

I told her about my dreams of living in Southern California and splitting my time between law, fighting, and even acting. We shared dreams together of what we could accomplish. She went with me to Tony Robbins seminars, and together we worked through some hard places in our childhoods. Someone who sees you in tears over loneliness and abandonment and doesn't think any less of you is just going to be part of your life in some way.

Molly was always loyal to me. When the NAC came after me and invented that doping scandal, Molly supported me unwaveringly. She wasn't clingy. When the opportunity arose for me to go to Big Bear, she pushed me to accept it.

For nine years, I knew that I could go to training camps, enjoy dinners and evenings with gorgeous women, come back to Reno, and find Molly there: stable, welcoming, faithful, and kind. And hot.

But eventually her dreams came between us. She had never lost her desire for hearth and home and the patter of little feet, and I got to feeling like I was keeping her from pursuing what she wanted and deserved. We broke up. It was the right thing to do for both of us. We wanted two different kinds of life.

After the Brinkley fight, the Valentine's Day massacre, I was in the middle of a career resurrection. Sponsors saw how much I could take without giving up. I may have lost, but I showed the mettle of my determination and will to win. That was attractive.

I also showed what I could do completely alone with no help and no encouragement. While I was working out at Big Bear, I'd been in disgrace with no promise of a comeback. I'd used that time profitably. What could I do with a slew of professional trainers, some funding, and a promise of hitting the big time? What could a motivated partner make out of me?

Suddenly sponsors started coming out of the woodwork. I was worth an investment. I had so much going on. Bold Management was looking at me. I had just gone down to LA and met with Freddy Roach, who agreed to train me. Manny Pacquaio was cleaning up at that time, and he was in their stable along with Amir Kahn. Amir invited me back to his apartment to spar. I got my SAG card with a view to getting back into entertainment somehow and planned to relocate permanently to LA. I was looking at apartments across from Freddie's Wild Card boxing club.

Proximity is such a huge part of success in LA. You have to be there to come to an audition minutes after you get a call. You have to be there to take a meeting if someone offers to connect you with a producer or a director or an agent. You can't live in another state and say, "Gee, thanks, but I'll see if I can fit you in next week." The whole business is fast and electric. You have to stay plugged in to feel the current.

I made a deal with my partners, because I had started my law practice by this time and brought some law school buddies in with me. I only wanted $2,500 a month from the practice. The guys could use my name and image and make as much money as they wanted. Anything above the $2,500 was theirs. I signed agreements with sponsors to bring me $5,000 a month.

The training camp my sponsors reserved for me was in Tampa; so I relocated there temporarily. I was in a condo on the beach, getting into the best shape of my life and increasing my skill and effectiveness exponentially. I worked all day and played at night. My best friends were professional athletes, and I lived the life they lived. It seemed that every good thing in life was on the table for me. Nothing was off limits. I was on my way up.

I went home to Reno for a visit and got a call from Molly. She needed to see me in person and talk. I have three sisters; I knew what was up. There was either a death in the family, or she was pregnant. Nobody in her family had said a thing about a death, and I was not stupid. So I prepared myself for the kind of conversation we were about to have.

When she came over and broke the news to me that the two of us had a new little life to consider, I congratulated her. "You're going to be a fantastic mother," I told her. "And I will be the best dad this kid could have. Neither one of you will ever lack for anything I can give you."

She could sense the "but" coming, because it was coming. If I'm anything, I'm honest. "I need you to know that this kid does not mean that we're getting back together. A kid does not change who we are or what we've both expressed that we want out of life. But I will be there for you. I promise you that."

When she left, I called my Dad. Warren was thrilled. "You're going to be such a good dad. This is the best news." I tried to respond in kind, but I felt betrayed. The Lieutenant Colonel knew me. He knew that a kid was not on my radar. I wanted him to mourn my foot-loose future, and here he was popping champagne.

I went back to Tampa and doubled down on the training. Molly was a realtor with a strong business. Sure, the market was terrible then. The housing bubble had burst, and a lot of people who had invested in rental properties couldn't find tenants who could pay to fill them. Mortgages were collapsing right and left. I lost property, as did several of my friends. Some of them were three deep in worthless houses. We joked with each other that we had gone from ballin' to fallen.

It wasn't a joke to Molly. She lost income. The house she had bought with money she had saved while she worked with her dad during college slipped out of her hands. She had to short sell it at a devastating loss.

Suddenly, she was pregnant, single, and living in a bedroom of her parents' house. Her business was not picking back up. She felt trapped and desperate.

So she called me. She laid it all on the table for me. I saw her situation through her eyes, and I called on that deep friendship that we had forged during ten years of dating. She didn't need me to be there for her with a blanket and diapers at the hospital. She needed me to be there for her now.

No matter what it cost me.

With that phone call, my life changed. My dreams curled up into a ball on my closet shelf to wait for some time in the future when I could unfold them again. LA was not a possibility. Maybe it hadn't been after the first phone call when I knew she was expecting.

My ambition was going to have to change for the time being.

I had run up against that first, vital conviction I had felt as a child. Dads are THERE for their kids. They don't consider themselves first. They don't parent from afar. They stay involved daily. They check in.

They care. They know little things about what the kid thinks and needs and loves and worries about.

I could not do that and stay a killer in the ring. I had not wanted to surrender my freedom, and maybe those last weeks in Tampa were a long goodbye to a life that I knew I could not have. I was going to have to open my heart and dive deep into those exhausted emotional wells.

So I called up and rented a house for Molly. I paid all her bills. I supported her and the child as soon as I knew that's what Molly needed from me. And I have done it every day since. Molly never needed to provide for herself, and I think that one of the greatest gifts I ever gave Aiella was her mother's complete time and attention. I will never regret that gift.

From the moment I knew my daughter was on her way, I understood that she also needed me, not just her mom, as much as she needed food and sleep. And no matter what her arrival changed in my life, she would never pay for the dreams I deferred with her own heart and mind and soul. She would not suffer either my absence or my grudging and unwilling presence.

I was going to be a good dad.

25 | **Preemption**

My last fight as a professional boxer took place in September 2010. Aiella was just a few months old, and I was still walking the line between my dreams of boxing domination and my responsibilities to my family and my businesses. But everyone in my life understood the prominence boxing occupied in my existence, and they expected my devotion to training and winning.

All that changed when I faced down Kassim Ouma at the Grand Sierra Resort.

I loved fighting at the GSR. It had been the scene of some memorable victories for me. Most recently, I had won against Billy Bailey and Anthony Bartinelli there. It was also a space that I was retaking. After all, my fight against Charles Howe, which had been rendered a no contest after the fact when the accusation fiasco hit, had taken place at the GSR. With every victory I won specifically at that same place, I put the pain and humiliation of the scandal further behind me.

For two months, I had trained like a beast for this fight. I was in the best shape of my life, with no injuries and no weaknesses to hold me back. I respected Ouma, his power and his talent, but I was confident when I entered the ring with my entourage in tow that I was heading for a third win in a row at the GSR; and if I won this fight, I would be in line to fight for the World Middleweight title.

The referee that night was my old friend and mentor Vic Drakulich. He had been refereeing for my matches since college, and he knew my father and most of my coaches. A tough old lawyer, I knew that he would be objective in his decisions, but all the same, it seemed like a good omen to see a familiar face.

Vic started us off, and I went to town. I was hitting Ouma with some good, hard shots. I could tell that the coaching and roadwork I'd put in were paying off. I was going to win. I could feel it. I looked across the ring and saw my sister Gina, my girl Molly, and my baby Aiella. My heart swelled with confidence and determination. I was going to win for them.

When the fifth round came, I was holding my own. Then, out of the blue, Ouma landed a headbutt that rang my bell. It did more than that. It knocked out my lights. I don't mean that I took a nap; I was still conscious. But I couldn't see a damn thing. Then I started seeing double.

That scared me. I can't tell you how much. I knew my capacity to withstand punishment. I could fight hurt. I could take the pain, put it somewhere it wouldn't bother me, and get the work done. But this was different.

If I couldn't see, I couldn't read. I couldn't drive. I couldn't intimidate an opponent in the courtroom.

My work as an attorney would be twice as hard.

I couldn't just go blind. What if this was permanent? What if I had finally suffered a real, debilitating injury? How would I take care of my daughter and my girl? I had just seen my sister's face across the ring. What if I never saw it again?

All these thoughts ran through my mind in seconds. I blinked and put my concentration back on what was happening around me. I heard Vic's familiar voice calling my name.

"Joey, get your hands up. Are you ready to fight?" he asked.

Staring straight ahead, I said, "Vic, I'm seeing double."

I could feel him pause, feel his worry in the air between us. But he was a professional, and he did what he had to do. "Joey, are you telling me you want this fight stopped?"

"Yes," I answered.

Right then, I knew what I meant in that answer. Yes, I wanted this fight stopped. I know that I would have to win multiple fights in order to be in line for a title fight. I had a brain scan done which confirmed that I had a major concussion. My Dad was deployed in Africa at the time of the fight but had just returned home. He sat me down and said, "Son, maybe it is time to quit the ring and go to your fall-back career you know—an attorney—before they are rolling both of us around in wheelchairs, drooling all over ourselves." So I agreed to leave the fight game behind and practice law.

I wanted to leave with my record and my dignity and my mental and physical powers intact. Fighting was important, but my daughter was more important. I wouldn't throw away my ability to care for her over this profession. My balance returned gradually after the fight, and I took that gift as a confirmation of my decision.

While I would keep boxing in my life in some way for the rest of my life, I would direct my energy into law. I was still a winner with an incredible record behind me and a world of opportunities in front of me. And now, I was going to win with the law degree and the bar certification that had cost me so much to obtain.

It was time to start Joey Gilbert Law.

From my experience with fight promoters, I knew that I wanted to do things differently in the realm of law. I didn't want to work my way up in some huge corporate firm, where my power to advance was in someone else's hands. I wanted to rely on myself to succeed and achieve. I wanted all the opportunity, and that meant taking all the risks.

I did all the paperwork to set up shop for myself legally in Nevada. So I had a firm, technically. But a firm needs clients, and those were exactly what I didn't have. It was time to get the idea factory in motion.

You know me by now. My idea factory runs on physical motion. I went for a run.

I get random ideas on runs. And this time while I was running, I saw a whole bunch of empty billboards. Because of the recession, a lot of businesses had closed.

Those who hadn't were cutting corners to save cash. They were cutting things like advertising.

In a way, that strategy made sense. Cut your losses. Conserve your outflow. Hang on for the next good time.

Here's the thing, though. People in Nevada were still getting in trouble. They still needed a lawyer. And I wasn't going to be their lawyer if they didn't know they could hire me. The potential client base existed. Now was the time to invite them all to my front door.

But I wanted to do that in a different way. Usually, billboard and bus stop advertisers put up a telephone number. But a lot of people busy driving by or walking in a hurry wouldn't copy a number. At least they wouldn't copy the right number. They might see the design, remember the name, and make a mental note to search the number later.

That's when it hit me. I wanted them to Google me. I couldn't just use the Google name for all kinds of reasons to do with copyright infringement, but I figured that Google didn't own the rainbow. It also didn't own every exact font close to its iconic shape.

I could tell people to Search Joey Gilbert Law, and I could put the word "Search" in rainbow colors that looked somewhere in the neighborhood of the Google word shape. That search was a money idea. I could smell it. And together with my gorgeous mug and boxing name recognition, papering Reno with my brilliant billboards seemed like a safe bet.

Let me be clear. It was still a bet. I was buying up a

lot of real estate that nobody else was using, and it was vacant for a really good reason. Times were bad. Well-established local law firms were hurting. Who was I as a newcomer to use an advertising strategy they'd all rejected to set myself in a winning position?

I was a champion, that's who.

Because it was hurting for income, just like the rest of the city, the advertising company cut me a great deal. I got those billboards for pennies on the dollar. And I locked them up for months in advance. I figured the deal helped both of us. I was getting unparalleled coverage across Reno, and the billboard company was getting some financial security. Win-win.

Boy, did those billboards work! Clients started flooding in, and I quickly had to hire staff to help me handle the influx. Citizens in a jam remembered to Search Joey Gilbert Law, and I got busy helping them.

The other law firms were not crazy about my approach, to say the least. Within my first year as an attorney, I had over ten bar complaints and was viewed as a disrupter in the space. I had zero convictions on my license, but I put a number of practices out of businesses. What can I say? I seized an opportunity that they let pass them by.

Let me tell you that I would not have grasped success as a new firm if I had not approached my need for clients from a position of consistency. Remember those lessons? Get up and get moving. Touch base with your goals and values. Keep swinging and push the pace. That's what I did. Those habits were a matter of course for me, and when I needed them, they worked.

My success as an attorney came from this incredible gamble with spending my life savings on billboards. And I would not have seen this chance if I had not been in the flow of consistency with my daily habits.

But winning once wasn't enough. Now that I owned the public attention, it was time to keep going. And to do that, I needed another great habit.

26 | Goal Writing

Here's something I know for sure: nothing good happens without focus.

If I'm going to remake my body into a fighting machine, I have to focus on that goal. And if I'm going to use that machine to rack up wins in the boxing matches I enter, I'm going to have to focus on that end result. Focusing on the end has a way of helping all of those intermediary steps fall into line.

It helps with daily, in-the-moment decisions, too. If I have a very clear goal in mind, then I can think about myself and my small choices in a very different way. Let's take the instance of a goal I have had in the past—opening a new branch.

If that goal remains a thought in the back of my head, it doesn't have much hope to reach completion. Speaking for myself, the back of my head is a pretty crowded place. For some of you, it may look like attic storage. For me, it looks like a New Year's Eve party.

So how do I get that goal out of the back of my head and out into the world? I've found a useful tool that I use regularly: goal writing. Now this tool is not new with me. In a way, every corporate mission statement, every family budget, every marriage vow is a kind of goal writing. The way I use it is not even unique to me (thanks, Tony Robbins).

What I'm telling you is that I use it, and it works. So that new branch I want to open? I put it down on paper. I put that paper where I can see it regularly. Sometimes I put it on my phone in a place where it's going to interrupt me, like my lock screen or my wallpaper.

Then it goes from the front of my mind to the back of my mind. It goes from the snack table at the party to the stage behind the DJ table. All the other thoughts start dancing to that music.

So when I already have a court case in the place where I want my new branch to be, I can look into real estate listings before the day and then go check things out in person when I finish my day in court. When I hire a new associate that really seems to get after his work and show some initiative, I start evaluating him or her quietly with the thought of putting that associate in charge of the new branch when I'm not there.

You see? Goal writing opens you up and narrows your focus at the same time. So you're more observant, but your observations work to a purpose.

You know how people say that you notice more about things that affect you? Like you buy a red Toyota, and then you see red Toyotas everywhere. Or you find out you're having a baby, and suddenly the world is full of strollers and bottles. That's just a thing that happens with everybody.

Goal writing gives you the power to harness this

thing that's already going to happen and make it work for you. It snatches unplanned moments and opportunities out of thin air and hands them to you.

It also helps with this sifting process that you do as you're growing into a fuller human being. You rethink your values and ideas from the bottom up. You dare yourself to ask harder questions.

Why do I think this value is important?

Why do I expect myself to reach this goal?

Is what I'm working to achieve really the most important thing to me?

Am I justified in this opinion that I hold?

Do objective facts support my perspective?

Who do I want to be in the world?

How do I want to be remembered by the people I love?

See, if you're not directing your energies in a specific way, you don't have to ask questions like that. You can just run with your family scripting and personal experience, throw your energy out randomly into the universe, and live with what happens. A lot of people are happy with throwing that kind of psychic spaghetti against the wall of time and seeing what sticks.

Not me. This one life is too precious to waste it on anything haphazard. I choose to use everything about myself, even my crazy ADHD energy and multi-faceted focus, to achieve a ridiculous level of success. Everything is on purpose.

You better believe I'm taking advantage of goal writing.

27 | Luxury

A lot of people dismiss luxury out of hand; it's just something they don't value. They see it as frivolous or vain. But I don't. To me, luxury communicates certain ideas to the people around me.

Luxury is part of my brand. People have certain expectations of me, certain qualities I've taught them to anticipate by exemplifying them. I look neat and clean. I smell like myself and no one else (really amazing, in other words!) People have said when I first walk into a room, before they even saw me, "I knew Joey was here because I smelled him!"

There's a story to that smell. I wear a particular Paris cologne. I was on stage once during a Paris fashion week (long story) with Naomi Campbell, and after the show, two guys in the industry came up to me and told me to come with them. They took me to a small Paris shop where the owner tested my skin and mixed a personalized fragrance just for me that works with my skin chemistry. I keep bottles of that stuff lined up in my closet so that I never run out.

One guy I knew came up to me and asked the name of the cologne I wear. I told him the story. "It's personalized, dude," I told him. "I don't know if it will work on you. No one smells like Joey Gilbert but me."

But his wife loved it. So he offered me a twelve thousand dollar marketing plan if I would put him in touch with the people. I accepted and got a killer marketing plan. Unfortunately, he got a cologne that wasn't made for him and didn't smell the same.

That's the whole point. Luxury says to people that you care about small details. That's an invaluable invisible message to give my clients and my opponents in court. They see the dimple in the tie and the gloss on the shoes, and they can assume that they will get a lawyer who is on top of his game, who has examined every argument and gathered every piece of evidence.

And you know what? They're right.

You see, I don't use luxury as a kind of cover-up, like painting over a water stain in a wall instead of fixing the plumbing behind the wall. I use luxury instead as a finishing touch to advertise the quality of the person I am. I do put a hundred percent of my effort into everything I undertake. I do take just as much care with each client and each new business strategy as I do with the care of my car, my physical body, my home, my office, and my wardrobe.

I always shine my shoes before I leave my house. I believe in that old saying, "Can't make that deal with a dirty heel." I will back up the car and go home if I realize I forgot an important detail like that. I will always be absolutely prepared to the smallest particular in every area. I think that this attention to the small points that mean so much when taken together is something that a lot of people miss.

My old mentor Sly Stallone always used to tell me about the difference between those that talk the talk and those who walk the walk. You can't talk about success if you don't look it. A put together appearance is all part of the package and the process, because finite details matter whether others want to acknowledge that fact or not.

And if we're going to be blunt, let me say two more things. Nice things make you feel happy and successful. Don't discount the effect of luxury in boosting optimism and confidence. Those qualities will show up in your work and in your personal life.

My last word on the subject? Luxury lets your clients and your colleagues know that you're not hurting. You're a successful person who can afford the small details because you're more than fine on the basics. Luxury telegraphs winning.

And I'm a winner.

PART 4

MOTIVATION

"

Let me tell you something you already know. The world ain't all sunshine and rainbows. It's a very mean and nasty place, and I don't care how tough you are, it will beat you to your knees and keep you there permanently if you let it. You, me, or nobody is gonna hit as hard as life. But it ain't about how hard you hit. It's about how hard you can get hit and keep moving forward; how much you can take and keep moving forward. That's how winning is done!

"

SYLVESTER STALLONE
(ROCKY BALBOA)

28 | **Patriotism**

With a Dad like the Lieutenant Colonel, you better believe that we respected America in our family. He'd been an adult during the Vietnam War, a war that drew sharp lines in this country between those who said the pledge and would shake a soldier's hand and those who preferred to take to the streets to advertise their outrage with this country. I grew up in a house that recognized those two different viewpoints and located me on the side of the flag, the uniform, and the idea of American greatness.

You know, though, if you've grown up and left your parents like I have, that your ideas about life and the big questions change and grow as you experience more. Sometimes you break away completely. Sometimes you carve your own image of the family gods.

Being who I am, I wasn't going to mimic the Lieutenant Colonel's taciturn, stolid respect for the nation exactly. Come on! I'm too loud and active for that.

My love for America was going to take root in this ADHD brain and this Italian muscle on this rocky, dry Nevada soil. Yeah, I learned the stories in school about George Washington and the lie, Daniel Boone and the Alamo, and General George Patton handing

Hitler his ass. Those kinds of stories gave me an idea of what America should be: honest, adventurous, and just.

I added to that schooling my own ideas about a fatherland as a kind of family. What do you expect from an Italian? America was in my blood, and I felt the same kind of bond to it that I felt for family. Family sticks together, like Poppy Aiello told me, even if you disagree and get mad, like I had when I couldn't return to Chicago. Family was where you belonged, no matter what. It was a source of pride and identity, one you never betrayed.

America was also a place where anything could happen. When you grow up in Reno, even part of the way like I did, you'd walk the mountains where miners staked claims and worked them. Some of them became crazy or homeless or maimed, and some of them got to be millionaires. It was a wild and glorious gamble, one that might reward you if you had the balls and the spine to stick with your dreams.

I still believe that about America. I rose to prominence on the power of my own back and fists, and I seized my moment to parlay that prominence into the law office that has made possible every other venture I've pursued. I made myself a nice little launchpad to rocket into the stratosphere of real estate, mining, cannabis, and a bunch of other enterprises that will bear their fruit in time.

And I know beyond question that the fact of being American had a hell of a lot to do with that success.

Because I'm American, I expect the freedom to do whatever I can that's legal to rack up the stacks and the accolades without some government sticking its nose in and its hand out. Because I'm American, I have the luxury to dream about what's possible without worrying about bombs dropping on my roof or soldiers knocking down my front door.

I have good reason not to worry about any of that shit.

Behind me stands every Revolutionary patriot that dumped tea in a harbor or stood in front of a British cannon. Behind me stands every Western pioneer that volunteered for hunger, heat, and danger to push America west to the sea. Behind me stands every average GI Joe that has gone a thousand different places to tell the tyrants and the dictators exactly where they could stick their twisted ambitions.

How could that not swell your chest and straighten your backbone?

Americans do some boneheaded things sometimes. Just Google "Florida man" and your birthday, and get ready to have the limits of your belief in what people will do stretched. And I can't even tell you how frustrated I've been in 2020 watching America make some decisions that never should have happened.

But that's our family doing weird shit. Who doesn't have some crazy uncle showing up at the weekend barbecue? We all do. We're family. And no matter how mad we get at each other, we stick together, like family does.

We've got great roots, a great family story. And we've got room to grow in splendor, pushing the boundaries of what we thought possible. I'm proud as hell to be a citizen of the United States, and I always will be.

That part of my identity motivates me to achieve more and push myself further. I may not have a West to conquer, but I have a self to conquer. I may not have an enemy soldier in front of me, but I have everyday injustice and ignorance in my own community to subdue. I can look to the patriots of the past and bring those values of honesty, adventure, and justice into my life now.

Land of my fathers? You bet your ass it is.

29 | Justice

You know what I love about handling a DUI case? I get to see someone at a low point, pick that person up, and open a door to a solid future. I get to change lives. It's the best job in the world.

Years ago, my buddy Clint, who works as my director of marketing, floated an idea past me. He's not going to believe I'm putting this story in print, because I like to bust his balls telling him I came up with it alone. But if you can't use your own book to give one of your best friends a little shout out, what's the point?

"You know, people get scared of the lawyer price tag," Clint told me.

"Yeah," I nodded. "What did you have in mind?"

"999," he answered. "It's almost a thousand, but it's not a thousand. It feels like less without that extra decimal. What if you offered a DUI defense for $999?"

"We could do that for the simple cases," I agreed. "Of course, more complicated ones, we'd have to add fees. But we could offer a base price."

"You're the killer with the billboards," Clint shrugged. "Going after the competition is kind of your thing."

"Fists up and keep moving," I grinned.

So, Joey Gilbert Law came up with the promotion

that became my bread and butter for a long time: $999 for a DUI defense. But I didn't want to offer just your run-of-the-mill DUI defense. I saw how inefficient those were, and I knew I could not only charge less but do a better job.

Here's how a DUI defense went down before I showed up. After a client got out of jail, he'd find a lawyer from the internet or a TV ad, or a friend or relative who wasn't hung over would find one for him. The client would show up at the lawyer's office, pay an installment towards some fees that were going to rack up quick, and get paperwork started with the court. The court date to get an evaluation or file a plea or anything with forward motion would get pushed out a few months.

Then, the client would show up for meetings (billable) and three to four different court appearances (billable) for which the lawyer would have to prepare (billable). All this time, the client was still in the same state of mind and life that had led to the first charge. Sometimes he'd rack up another DUI before the first was adjudicated. Sometimes he'd rack up two.

Finally, the client would show up to court where something was going to happen. The State of Nevada would present a competent prosecution, and the defense would try to get a decent deal, like a suspended sentence instead of jail time. The suspended sentence meant that the client had thirty, sixty, or ninety days to complete a checklist of pretty much the same standard tasks and pay a court fee in order to avoid jail time. Fail or skip, and the client would end up behind bars.

The checklist was pretty onerous taken all at once. Starting off with a first offense, you could face a thousand dollars in fines. On top of that, you had to complete an alcohol awareness program. Then perhaps you'd be ordered to get a psychological evaluation, do community service, and get an ignition interlock device to lock down your car if your blood alcohol level was over the limit. That's a hell of a lot to do and to pay in thirty days. Could you do it?

Cha-ching, cha-ching, cha-ching. That checklist wasn't going to come cheap, and the court wasn't going to be nice and patient if you screwed it up. Subsequent offenses were going to increase in fines and jail time. A DUI could mess up your life for a long time, leading to job and home loss and maybe relationship failure. And all that time, the lawyer was going to keep careful track of all those billable hours and make sure he got his before the State of Nevada got its fees.

I felt that we could do better in Nevada. I was already on a self-directed rotation of meeting with all the judges in the state. I wanted to ask them for the benefit of their wisdom and experience. I figured that if anyone could tell me how to win in front of them, it was them.

Now I added discussions of DUI cases to those meetings. I floated ideas past some justices. I saw that most of them wanted the same thing out of the law that I did: justice. We all agreed that the current system was more punitive than just. But I saw that the law could be made to work for the good of society and the client with a few tweaks.

Understand me clearly: I was not going to these justices to grease the wheels so that they'd take it easy on my clients. My daughter is out on these roads. My mother is out on these roads. I don't want any unstable drunk drivers out there getting off easy and continuing to put people in danger. I want dangerous drivers off the roads. At the same time, I want people on the wrong path in life to get the help they need.

I told you about all those Tony Robbins courses. Years ago, I had become a certified coach with his program. I knew I had the motivational skills to intervene and make a difference in the life of someone who had reached a tipping point.

Out of my independent review of the system, my meetings with the judges, and my understanding of human motivation, I created a method to handle DUI cases swiftly, efficiently, and humanely, with a net outcome that achieved safety on the roads and a stable life for the client. Oh, and it also happened to be profitable. Everybody wins.

Here's what happens when a client walks through my door. My staff welcomes the client courteously and respectfully, and then the client pays that $999 fee. Afterwards, I meet with the client personally. During this meeting, we come to an understanding.

I outline the program. If I sense a willingness to pursue that program, we're off to the races. I have my staff make an appointment with an evaluator and get the rest of the wheels in motion. If I sense resistance, I push back some. I get the client to see an evaluator that day or the following day to hear the truth about his or her relationship with alcohol. If there's a softening and admission of need, then we're back where we were on track. If not, I wash my hands of the client.

People tend to get mad and act out when I boot them out of my office. But I don't even have to post up. I can smile, ask them to Google me and meet me in the parking lot if they're that upset, and otherwise, get their hind parts off my designer furniture. I don't have time or energy to waste on people who don't want to change. Let them find another lawyer to do things the old way.

Once I've got a compliant client sitting across from me, we have a heart-to-heart about how things could go if they follow my advice. Their future doesn't have to include jail or a ruined life. But it will involve a lot of hard work and change.

First, I push the court date out four to six months. My clients need time to work through that checklist, and I want to give it to them. Usually, I recommend that the client get an evaluation whether the court's going to require one or not. It's mentally and emotionally useful for helping someone come to terms with what's up and start the work of moving away from alcohol abuse. So is the DUI course. The client starts attending that.

Because my fee is out of the way and I'm not collecting any further funds, I have the client proactively start saving monthly toward the court fees, a couple hundred bucks a month. I also have the client start community service, an average of forty hours. For clients who are strapped for cash, we up the community service hours and do the best we can with the savings. Double the service is awesome, and it's doable if you start early enough.

When I show up to court with my client for the first time, the client has every item on the checklist complete. The State of Nevada produces the facts in the case. Then it's my turn.

"Your Honor, yes, the facts in the case entitle the State to demand jail time from my client. But this client, as you can see before you in the file, Your Honor, has completed the DUI One course and submitted to the hundred-dollar evaluation, even though that was not required by the court. My client has put time and effort into remediating the circumstances that led to the initial offense, and at this point, jail time would only derail the significant progress that's been made.

"Also, Your Honor, if you'd note the eighty hours of community service, I'd like to discuss my client's finances, which are straitened. If the court would see fit to take into account the evaluation fee and the extra community service in a reduction of the fine, the client would appreciate the court's lenience.

"Your Honor, you can gather from the file that what you see before you is a changed person who has used the time before today in a profitable way and has posed no further danger to the community. I ask that we dispense with the jail time, allow the client to pay a reduced fee today, and close the case with no further action."

Now the State of Nevada looks like a real prick if it still demands jail time from someone who's turned things around that far.

Ninety-nine percent of the time, I show up to court once with a person who is going to say sorry, show progress, pay a fine, and walk out completely done with the whole thing. My clients don't go to jail. My clients don't rack up other offenses and ruin their lives. My clients get help, get better, and pay their debt to society in advance and with a good attitude. I think that helps everybody.

The way I run my firm shows the way I think the law should work. It should motivate people to stop their various methods of assholery and get positive. On a larger scale, the more people the law stops and changes, the better we as a community and a state get. The thought that I can do that, make that kind of difference in someone's life, is a huge reason why I devote so much passion and energy to the law. I'm changing the place I live for the better every time I walk into my office.

Boom.

30 | **Fatherhood** *(Part 3)*

Fatherhood in reality was a learning experience for me. I constantly had to balance what I knew in my heart my kid needed against what I had to do to make our life successful. Yes, I got the message at a heart level that this kid loved me unconditionally and needed me absolutely. I also got the message at a head level that I had to be away to chase the dreams that were still attainable for me.

Like everyone predicted I would, I fell in love at first sight of that brown hair, huge eyes, and wrinkled face. My chest felt like the Grinch at the end of the Christmas special, bursting out of my ribs. I wondered how I had ever gotten along in a world where my daughter didn't exist. I knew I would do anything for her and thank fate for the opportunity to prove myself.

Those opportunities didn't come my way for a while. When my daughter was small, the lion's share of the care fell to Molly. Just practically, Aiella slept a lot, and I couldn't nurse her. I was also super busy caring for my baby law practice.

I was present when I could be present. And when I was there with Aiella, I was involved and loving. I changed diapers. I tucked her in. I gave hugs and piggyback rides.

This complete attention didn't happen all the time, of course. Looking after a needy little person is exhausting, and sometimes it was too much. My natural restlessness got the better of me from time to time, as it does with all new parents, I expect. At first it was hard to reconcile pre-baby Joey with post-baby Joey. I escaped to my phone, to the gym, to the countryside for a run—anything to feel like myself again. But the draw of that tiny piece of me learning to live at home kept drawing me back.

Molly was the one who did the majority of the feeding and carrying and carting around. She was the one who arranged playdates and doctor's appointments, the one who did the shopping and cooking and cleaning. She was a fantastic mom, just like I told her she would be. She gave our kid a hundred percent of herself, and our kid thrived under the attention and care.

I grew to love the ways I could share myself with Aiella. The first way was with her name. I changed the last letter of my grandfather's name, Poppy Aiello, to honor him with my first child. As much as he had poured into my life, he deserved a legacy from me. And giving my kid his name was a way of claiming her for clan Gilbert. It was a message out loud that Aiella belonged to my heart.

We were so close at heart that she couldn't bear to be away from me. Every tear that fell from that little girl's eyes when we said goodbye cut me deep. We called days "sleeps." I'd tell her, "Daddy's only going to be away for two sleeps," but she would wail just the same as if I'd said two years. I hated seeing her sad.

She taught me so much. She reinforced to me how right I'd been when I understood the devotion that fatherhood would require of me. All the sacrifice and love and time that I knew I would need to give a kid I now saw I did indeed need to give that kid. If anything, I might have underestimated how completely our lives would intertwine.

But I'd been wrong about those depleted wells. The love in her eyes and her smile filled me up in ways I hadn't anticipated. Knowing that I was responsible for such an amazing human arriving on the planet made me proud and happy. Seeing how she looked up to me expanded my capacity to achieve and endure. I could do anything in part because Aiella believed that I could do anything.

You want motivation? Seeing the trust in a kid's eyes is probably the most significant motivation around.

My daughter also taught me the connection I would have forever to Molly. I saw her in a new way not only as a friend and lover but also as a significant partner in the best thing I would ever do: parent this child. No change to our relationship then or after could ever change our roles as co-creators of a masterpiece. We were bonded for life. At our girl's graduation, wedding, promotions, and birthdays, we would stand side by side as long as we both lived.

Being a father has changed me completely from the scared kid who shrank from the possibility of failing at the enormously important role of parenthood. Once it was a reality of my life, I knew I couldn't fail at being a father. It was too important. I had to succeed—I was going to succeed—because my kid was counting on me.

31 | **Support Veterans**

Some of the situations I see trouble me greatly, especially when they seem so easily preventable. If someone had reached out for counseling, if someone had involved other people in what was going on in a home, if a child had confided in a teacher, if someone had chosen to treat their sadness with a hard run or a punching bag instead of a substance—if, if, if—then things might have been different.

I feel so much empathy for people I meet at the tail end of a string of bad decisions, especially when the beginning of that string goes deep into a matter of public responsibility. Do you know how many offenders are victims of child abuse? Do you know how many fatherless boys end up in gangs? Do you know how many women involved in sex work grow up as victims of domestic violence?

I do.

I especially hate to see preventable tragedies occurring in the homes of our veterans. Look, these guys give up a lot in service to the rest of us. As a citizen, you don't have to pick up a gun and hunt down bad guys who want to come here and detonate a dirty bomb, because they're doing it for you. You don't have to leave your family for months at a time. You don't have to risk injury and death. You don't have to eat the bad food, endure the bad weather, or learn to do without sleep for days at a time. You don't have to deal with any of that danger or suffering, because our veterans are standing in your place.

So as citizens, we all owe them big time. We owe them outstanding health care and professional counseling. We owe them the opportunity to integrate back into life here in the healthiest way possible.

Some guys do this naturally. I meet guys every day who came out of military service mentally strong and morally stable. These guys are fantastic husbands, dads, and employees. But some guys need some help getting to that level.

You should understand that war is a pressure cooker. It's a magnifying glass. It's a kiln. Whatever goes in comes out more itself than it was at the beginning. In that way, it's like deep grief or a high-stress job.

Every Warfighter starts life as a child. As that child grows, it's building an emotional, mental, and psychological framework for the rest of life. Think of it like a house. Some life constructions happen with great foresight, care, and integrity. Those kids grow up resilient and able to handle pressure and shock. Some life constructions happen haphazardly, with negligence, abuse, and trauma. Those kids grow up wounded and less able to bear further tragedy unless they heal properly first.

Many veterans enlist at the tail end of childhood, at

17 or 18, when their brains haven't fully developed. As newly minted adults, their psyches plunge into daily turmoil and terror. It's like those houses, those life constructions, get flooded and shaken by earthquake. The ones who were built well or who took time to repair before the devastation can withstand it much better than the ones who didn't have the same foundation.

But we can't control how a Warfighter enters military service. What we can do is take care of the ones who return to us. We can help fix the damage done in service to all of us. And those of us in the business of law and justice can advocate for proper treatment instead of punishment when the system of transition breaks down and our veterans deal with trauma badly.

Personally, I represent veterans pro bono whenever I can. Our veteran clients could have never afforded our services or the services of any private attorney. So we stand up for them because they stood up for us, and we count ourselves honored to have done so. It's a privilege to represent a veteran of our Armed Forces. When I see someone in trouble who is fully disabled due to PTSD and other combat injuries sustained in his deployments, I see an opportunity to introduce some hope and care into a troubled situation.

Look, everyone, our veterans need better care. They need more expedited services, counseling, additional career training, and the support they deserve. Too many are left to figure things out on their own. They are self-medicating. They are not dealing properly with their problems or the issues they are facing. This is not how we should be treating our nation's airmen, soldiers, sailors, and Marines. It's time to start doing more.

Our servicemen and women are coming home in droves with problems centered around PTSD, and they need better support. It will potentially get worse before it gets better. So please do what you can, and get involved with our veterans. Ask your local VA or veteran's support organization how you can be of use. Maybe you can't pay legal fees, but you could volunteer at a fundraiser to pay for medical expenses or prosthetics. Maybe through your own industry, you could come up with an equally creative way to support veterans.

Whatever you can do, do it. It's a small price to pay for the freedom you enjoy.

32 | **Leadership**

When the news first broke that people around the
world were getting massively sick and dying in hospitals, I felt for them as much as the tragedy-whore,
twenty-four-hour news cycle ever lets me feel for one
thing before it shoves another disaster in my face. I
wonder how many of you have started to feel exhausted, like I do, with so much misery around the world.
It's frustrating to be presented with need after need
without the ability to make a real difference.

What I generally feel, when I hear about worldwide
misfortune, is a mixture of impatience and sadness.
Listen, there are things ordinary people should be
able to do to make the world better. Natural disasters?
Sure, let's gather around, join forces, and donate to
the Red Cross. But human misery caused by oppres-
sive governments or terrorists? People on the ground
shouldn't put up with that crap. Kill the bastards and
make a decent place for your kids. Where are their
George Washingtons?

And if I expect this from other people, I sure as hell
expect it from me. Is my own government getting a
big head, stepping out of line, and taking power from
ordinary citizens? Is the government telling American

voters what kind of medical treatment they can get or how they can make a living? No way is that happening. No way am I standing aside and letting that happen.

We could all understand the first shelter-in-place order. If the horses are out of the barn, let's get them back and lock them up tight. But when the orders kept coming and coming and businesses started closing because they had lost an untenable amount of income after being ordered not to operate—that's when things got ridiculous. After a certain point, when enough horses have left the barn and it becomes clear that they have headed for the hills and started their own horse colonies, you have to deal with a society full of horses.

If you pay attention to history, and at this point you'd better, then you know what finally stopped the 1920 influenza pandemic: herd immunity. Yep, folks, human animals still need exposure to viruses in order to develop antibodies. Before we had a vaccine, that was only going to happen from getting the damn thing and getting over it.

We were never going to get through this thing with an extended quarantine. The only thing that a quarantine could do, after the initial horse-chasing few weeks when we had a shot at locking it up, was hurt people. Once that virus spread across the nation, we had to deal with the situation at hand.

How do we do that? We take the measures we can in order to get stronger and to follow the advice of doctors who are having success treating symptoms. That's all you can do with a virus: treat symptoms so that they don't damage your body permanently, and then strengthen your body to outlast the pathogen attacking it. We all know this. We've all dealt with a virus like this one before: chicken pox.

Any kid growing up the time I did, or before, knew that you were going to suffer through the hell that is chicken pox once in your life. Fever, itching, sores: that was going to happen to you. Now that we have a vaccine, kids may skip it or get a milder case. But in the prehistoric times when I was bouncing around Chicago, parents held pox parties as soon as one kid got infected. They figured it was going to make the rounds sooner or later, and it might as well be sooner. I shared lollipops with an infected kid. My mom handed me the paper stick. On purpose.

Did this mean our parents didn't care about us? No! They gave us ibuprofen to cool our fevers, oatmeal baths and calamine daubs to soothe the itching, and chicken soup and tea to dose us with protein and hydrate us. They had the common sense not to let our fevers rage out of control and damage our young brains permanently, not to let us scratch ourselves raw and damage our skin forever. They loved us, but they knew that sometimes Mother Nature is a real bitch that you can only appease until she decides to leave on her own.

I was stunned to see and hear grownup people and free Americans talking about staying home and shuttering businesses for months. Who had the cheddar stashed away to deal with that kind of closure? I knew from talking about finances regularly and in detail with my clients that average people in this country did not. So, who was going to make up the difference? Uncle Sam.

The problem was that Uncle Sam did not have bottomless pockets. In fact, that old credit addict was deeper in debt than a blind fish at the bottom of the Atlantic. The real people on the hook for a year's quarantine for the nation would be Aiella and her elementary school pals and their kids and grandkids. And with the government yanking back personal freedoms with the smug entitlement of a playground bully, the government wasn't going to make it easy from this point on for anyone to earn enough to pay its tab and get the nation back to solvency.

How could I sit back and let the government ruin people's lives now and ruin Aiella's life in the future? I couldn't stomach that. So, I got moving and learning and acting to stop the runaway train that was the government high on Coronavirus.

The first thing I did was research a workable treatment plan to deal with symptoms. I found out about doctors who were using a regimen of Hydroxychloroquine (an anti-malaria treatment) along with Azithromycin (Z-Pack) and Zinc Sulfate. No one who used those medicines in combinations died. I laid in a supply for myself, my family, and my close associates. I wasn't going to lose anyone to this thing.

I was soon glad that I had. My parents came down with Covid and grew seriously ill. I got them the medications fast and instructed them how to use them. Though they had a rough time for a while, they were not hospitalized and are still with me, knock wood.

That recovery spurred me to spread the word to the public. I wasn't a doctor, but I had found something that worked. It would be selfish and wrong not to share what I knew. All three drugs were so benign that they'd been prescribed to pregnant women for years. They weren't some out-there, experimental crapshoot.

The backlash that I got astounded me. People objected that the medications hadn't passed medical review in this context. Seriously? We didn't have the time for that kind of timidity. The current feedback from qualified professionals was that it was working.

This medicine should be made available to anyone who wanted it, but especially to all law enforcement, fire, first responders, and all health care professionals—if they want it. I'm not in favor of anyone forcing any medicine on anybody, but those who want it should be able to get it. And those forced into contact with the public should get it first.

Liability, you say? Have them sign a freaking waiver and give them some peace of mind! Are we not adults? Can we not make our own healthcare decisions?

I also was sickened by objections on the basis of class and race. I believed strongly that no matter who you are or where you come from or what your immigration status is, you should be provided this medicine and these medicines by the County/City immediately if you have a positive test for Coronavirus. There was even a way to do this codified in statute. Both the City of Reno and Washoe County had the power under this emergency to provide this care; they just needed to act.

How the hell else were people with a language barrier or no insurance or no doctor and no contacts in this town or going to acquire these lifesaving medications and not infect others or put the community at risk? Being sent home to tough it out just did not seem fair. At all. To any of us.

It's one thing not to want the government to pay for a year of vacation for the populace. It's another not to issue the means to stop symptoms and stop the spread quickly so that we can get back to business. Of course we should pay for the medicines and get them out there. What's the government for if not to make sure its citizens don't die preventable deaths?

I knew that we would overwhelm our hospitals if we didn't figure this part out quickly, because people would wait until the very end when they were too sick to help before they showed up to the hospital, massively contagious and likely beyond saving if they ended up on a ventilator. Ventilators were not the answer. The directives given by our government and health care professionals and the medications mentioned above were!

I advocated for testing in the livestock events center parking lot by the health care angels in the bug suits.

They could use the same space for handing out medication. We had the place, the power, and the resources. All that we needed was a little public leadership and positivity.

In a time of shortages on everything from toilet paper to hand sanitizer to basic baking goods, the real shortage we faced was leadership.

Instead of saying, "This drug cocktail might not be the final solution, but it's the best course of action for now," the leadership in Nevada shut down availability. Instead of realizing, "Hey, the virus has already spread throughout our society. Let's take steps to keep our economy going and help people too sick to work," our government forbade businesses to operate and ordered people to stay home. Instead of uniting the state with a strong, positive message of hope and forward motion, the government abandoned any real help and just told people to hunker down and hope for the best.

We were in a war for our lives, and our government was shrugging and looking for the exit.

Hell, no. That was not going to happen while I was still breathing. The people of this state needed a fighter, and lucky for them, that's exactly what I am.

33 | Liberty

Let me tell you something that motivates me big time: red tape. If I can see from point A to point B, you better have a fantastic reason for telling me I can't get there. If your only reason is, "Because I said so," and your name is not Warren Gilbert, you and I are going to have a huge problem.

I have seen my fill of red tape over the Coronavirus pandemic. All the restrictions, whether they're just annoying or whether they're costing lives and livelihoods, have made me feel like a bull being baited by a matador: red flags everywhere I look. Just let me say that you don't want to be the matador in that situation.

Pretty quickly after I started speaking up publicly about the hydroxychloroquine treatment, people started contacting me for help. Because I had a reputation as a fighting lawyer, and because I was taking a stand about getting people help, those who were suffering under restrictions came to me. I heard stories from ordinary people and small business owners that you would not believe.

Salons were not allowed to operate, and those who ran them had no recourse. Salon owners who had sunk a life savings into their businesses were shut down and going bankrupt, through no fault of their own. Bars and restaurants were severely limited and losing more money than they could stand. What had they done wrong to be losing everything? In America?

The worst part for me was the treatment of churches. I was raised Catholic, and church was a huge part of my growing up. Religious services formed a reliable pattern for my life, just as the doctrine and worldview provided a solid foundation for my perspective.

I knew how meaningful it had been in times of trouble for me to know that the church was there. When my grandparents died, the church led us in the familiar rituals that provided comfort to sustain our family. To know that in this time of fear and despair the government was preventing the church from offering comfort and healing to its parishioners enraged me.

Fortunately, I didn't have to sit in my office and stew about what was going on. I practiced a profession that could make a difference. So I launched a multi-pronged attack on the SpongeBob NannyPants government that was micromanaging medical decisions for adult human people.

Nevada governor Steve Sisolak had filed an injunction prohibiting the sale of hydroxychloroquine. I filed a lawsuit challenging his authority to infringe on the bodily autonomy of American citizens.

Sisolak also closed businesses. I filed lawsuits challenging his authority to rob American citizens of the right to earn a living.

I also went the public information route, spreading

knowledge about what the OSHA inspectors serving businesses with closure notices were and were not allowed to do. I advised people for free on what questions to ask these inspectors, what answers to give, and what actions to take.

I traveled the state attending public meetings advising community groups on how to fight unjust restrictions in their areas. People tried to negotiate with me, thinking that I was going to charge them hourly rates that they couldn't afford. Hell, no. I was Paul Revere telling Nevada citizens to wake up and get armed with the facts. Old Paul didn't charge, and neither would I.

I lost money on these lawsuits and fights. I lost time that I could have spent on my own business and my family. I lost sleep working for the people.

That was okay with me. It was a price I was willing to pay. I couldn't stand by and watch America change into something I no longer recognized.

One by one, I saw judges decide in our favor. Common sense and the promise of the Declaration that we could pursue life, liberty, and the pursuit of happiness in America won out. By Christmas, churches were welcoming parishioners again.

I'm looking around today at a Nevada where people can decide with their doctors on what treatments to take without government meddling. I'm looking around at a Nevada where small business owners can keep their doors open and their employees at work. I'm looking around at a Nevada where freedom of religion is no longer in question. I'm looking around at a bunch of grateful faces and healthy, happy citizens. And I feel pretty damn good about how I spent the last year of my life.

One thing I learned in life is that you never give up, no matter the odds. Stay in there, no matter how hard the fight is or how hopeless the outcome appears. If what you're doing is right, keep doing it.

Your liberty demands your sacrifice.

34 | Dreams

Let's talk about dreams. Most of us have some kind of burning ambition, something you're really attracted to doing or becoming. And yes, if you put all of your will and your mind and your heart into achieving what you want, you can make your dreams come true. But it doesn't always look like you think it will.

You know the dream I had when I was a kid: becoming the next Jerry Maguire. Man, that dream was perfect for me! I'm an athlete; so I've been where Cuba Gooding, Jr. was, shouting at somebody to show me the money. I'm naturally energetic and outgoing. I love people! So negotiations energize me. And I have that handy-dandy law background that lets me ninja my way through contracts. You could not come up with a more perfect career for me.

So I took the time a few years back to get the materials to study for the NFL agents exam for their industry licensure. I worked really hard on preparing for that exam. It reminded me of the time I spent getting ready for the bar.

I flew out to Washington, DC to take that exam. And after the amount of time and effort I put into study, I was sure that I would pass. I walked into that exam room confidently. After all, hadn't I worked at this dream for decades, not just the last few months? Hadn't my entire life been preparing me to face this examination? There was just no way I could fail.

Except that I did.

Let me tell you, it was hard to get those results back. It was hard facing up to the shame I felt at disappointing the people around me who had been excited for me, but most of all disappointing myself. How could I not come through for myself? How could I let myself down like this and waste the huge investment I'd made?

So the plane ride home was pretty gloomy. I've endured some dark times, and I know what that feels like. I also know that I can't sit with it for too long. The sharp outlines of the mountains and the clear, dry tang of the air in my home state helped me know what to do with my frustration, sadness, and loss.

Like I do most times when I'm upset, I used exercise as my personal Xanax. There's something about a long run for a couple of hours that lets me think clearly at the same time it pumps all kinds of endorphins into my system. It's good all around.

I thought back over the ways I'd been pursuing this dream up until now. What came to mind was my friend Kelly. I checked with her to make sure that she didn't mind my sharing her story. Kelly and I had met close to the time of *The Contender*, before the drug allegation fiasco. She was friends with a good friend of mine, and she said to me, "Come to Jiu Jitsu. It'll be good for you." So I started coming for a little while, and we became good friends. Anybody who was really there for me at my lowest point became a close friend.

Unfortunately, Kelly had gone through a divorce from her husband of fourteen years. They ran a martial arts studio together. When she left, she left everything behind in Reno, planning never to return.

Kelly started fighting MMA, and I was doing my camp to prepare for my fight with Kassim Ouma, what turned out to be my grand farewell to professional boxing. I brought in two guys who were sprinters and a personal trainer there as well. As Kelly and I were both preparing for professional fights, we did our camp together. We were in Tahoe, which involved elevation training, including a lot of running and sprints at altitude - uphill with weight vests. That kind of work is no joke! And Kelly kept up with us.

She was two weeks out from her fight, while I was about eight weeks out from mine. She came in on that last week and just jumped in with us. Then she had her fight, and all of us from the camp came to watch.

I saw something special in Kelly when I saw her fight. I'd seen her train, and I knew the kind of grit and determination she poured into training. It turned out that her preparation translated into a fiery will to win when she got into the ring. I knew as soon as I left the audience that night that I needed to invest in Kelly. She was too talented to stop now.

I knew that Kelly was loyal and that the divorce had

taken a lot out of her, including her dreams of running a martial arts studio. She had just finished a huge task preparing for that fight and seeing it through, and now she was at loose ends. Odds were that she was going to end up back with her ex-husband, which would not have been healthy for her. She needed to do something to focus her energy and attention, and I knew she could do well at a fight career. So, I got her out of Reno.

After that fight, I made a phone call to my bro Diego Sanchez, who had been there for me up in Big Bear during my suspension. Diego was training at Greg Jackson's in New Mexico. He's where Holly Holm trained, Donald Seroni, Cowboy John Jones, all of these fighters. I told Diego how much potential Kelly had, and I found out that they could give her a trial and put her through her paces if I got her down there soon.

I told Kelly, "You should pursue fighting. You're great at it! Try it, or at least just get away for a while, hit the reset button." I could see a gleam of hope in her eye, one that clouded once she started thinking about plane tickets and travel costs. So I just took care of that. I could, and it was a little thing to me, while it would be a big thing for her, maybe a prohibitive thing.

I flew down with her to New Mexico to try out for Jackson's. It happened to be a Jiu Jitsu day, which was good for her. Remember, that's how we got to know each other. I knew she was a badass at Jiu Jitsu. After that portion, the athletes there were running sand dunes, which was kind of a popular thing that Jackson's athletes do.

By the way, Diego got me good right then. I had come out dressed nicely, as I usually am, with a thousand-dollar pair of shoes and jeans and a nice shirt. In other words, I hadn't planned on hitting the ring that day, let alone the dunes! But I couldn't leave a challenge behind, so I started running up the sand dunes, too! I think they kind of underestimated that Reno has elevation as well, because they thought maybe that Kelly would break on the dunes. But she didn't!

At the end of the trials, Greg Jackson asked Kelly to be a part of the team, helping to train Julie Kedzie, who was one of the pioneers of women's MMA. Julie was getting ready for a fight. So Kelly actually flew back to Reno, grabbed some stuff, went back, and helped her with her fight. Kelly moved to New Mexico and stayed for another year and a half before she came back to Reno. While she fought professionally, Kelly chose me to act as her agent, arranging all her fights between 2010 and 2012.

When I was talking to Kelly in preparation for this book, I asked her about that time. She told me this: "That pivotal moment changed my life. It changed the course of everything I did from that day forward, setting me towards a positive outcome. I really think that if I would have stayed here, it wouldn't have been healthy for me. I'm so grateful for that moment. I would do anything for you, Joey, just like I know you would do anything for me."

She's right. She's a true friend, and you don't skimp when true friends and family need you. A huge motivation for me is helping others achieve their dreams.

All that to say, when I got back from Washington and started running, I thought about Kelly. For her and for others, I had already done most of the practical work an agent does: finding fights, arranging training, getting the proper testing and weigh ins done, getting venues and negotiating details with them. You might not realize from the spectator end the incredible amount of work that goes into a fight.

I had started a promotions company back when I was still boxing full time. That company was still operating full strength. Brett Summers, Clint Cates, Drew Kachurak, and my girl Molly were going strong with that venture. They did a lot of the detail work, leaving me free to show my people the money, like I always wanted to do.

On that run, I realized that in the most important ways, I had already fulfilled that dream. My little kid self could sit back and smile, because I was Jerry Maguire in all the ways that mattered. No, I didn't have that license from the NFL. Maybe someday I would take another stab at it. But that piece of paper was not what would say that I fulfilled my dreams. I was the judge of whether that had happened for me, and it had. I could find motivation in that satisfaction.

I was able to let go of the bad feelings that had haunted me on the plane ride back and step right back into my life and the many pursuits that were filling my heart and mind with happiness. I could look for new ways to bring my dream to fruition over and over again.

A lot of times we set up barriers to accomplishment without even realizing what we're doing. We say, "Well, I have to reach this step before I can move on to that one." And maybe some of those steps are just not necessary.

So I would encourage you to take a step back from your dreams every once in a while and think about the difference between process and achievement. You may not need to climb every step on the staircase you've outlined to the next level. Maybe you jump over a few steps. Maybe you realize that you're already at the level in your sights in a lot of ways.

Dreams come true in a lot of ways, and they don't always look like you think they will. Learn to recognize them when you see them walking around in your waking life.

35 | Government

Growing up as a little kid, government was something I could take for granted. The huge face of the US government to me was living in my house, after all. As long as Warren Gilbert was on the job, the government to me seemed responsible, efficient, morally upright, and dangerous to its enemies. I needed to look no further to feel good about being an American.

And the eighties and nineties were a pretty pro-government time to grow up. I wasn't old enough to know about Vietnam and the Carter malaise, which were in the rearview mirror and unlikely to come into conversation. I was old enough to watch World War II and John Wayne movies. Between Patton and the Duke, I thought the American soldier was pretty much the paragon of all that was right in the world.

Reagan mania, which swept through our pro-military small town, only reinforced that view. And then you had Rambo and GI Joe. It seemed a foregone conclusion everywhere I went that the American form of government was hands down the best in the world. Who would even question that fact?

As you grow up, you learn things that make you question your assumptions. You learn about ways the government has disappointed its people, things it should have done better. For some of those actions, you feel shame and responsibility.

If I could go back and erase the stain of racism and slavery from our country, I would do it in a heartbeat. I hold people from all kinds of backgrounds dear to my heart. I hate that their ancestors were in many cases misused by the people running the country at that time.

I live out west, and the history of Native American conflict, genocide, and resettlement is very present here. It's a complicated history, but one that we can't ignore. Looking around at the incredible natural beauty and peace of this part of the country, you can't help but feel sorrow for the people who lost that land. You can't help but wonder how America could have done things differently.

Those faults are true, and we as Americans can own them and do better in the present and future without throwing the whole American experiment away as a bad job. With all the pain, there is real excellence and worth in our government. We can't turn away from what is good without doing ourselves and the world a grave disservice.

Nowhere in the world has equaled the durability, fairness, goodness, and plain common sense of our founding documents. The men who wrote them for us were flawed human beings, yes, but they were also courageous patriots with stunning minds and a prescient sense of what this nascent country would need as it grew. They built an awe-inspiring mansion for us to inherit and occupy. No amount of renovation or redecoration that we find necessary over the years can negate the fact that the house of our government was built soundly.

As I've gotten older and seen more of the world, I've understood my part in this country more and more clearly. I've come to understand that we don't just sit back and moan that the shingles are falling off and the lawn needs mowing. We roll up our sleeves, get out there, and do what needs to be done. This country belongs to us. That doesn't mean we should be looking for home equity loans. It mean we should be spending our nights and weekends fixing the place up.

Okay, enough with the metaphors. You get what I'm saying, right? We all need to own our government. It's a good government, one that will last us centuries into the future if we take care of it. But we need to take care of it. It's my job, and it's your job.

People get so caught up in divisive national politics that they don't see the power of getting involved closer to home. Nobody really needs to hear your hot take on how the president should have handled some policy question. You know what people need? They need you to show up at city council meetings and speak on local ordinances. They need you to campaign for mayors and state senators who are in touch with the people's thoughts more than the people's purse strings.

What happens close matters most.

Look, when all this Covid restriction started coming down the pike, I saw that the people of my city and my state needed my help first. Alabama and New York and everywhere else were going to have to rely on their own citizens and elected representatives. But the people of Nevada were my business. They were living in my room of the America house, so to speak, and I needed to pay attention to the holes and cracks in my own room.

That's why I acted fast and decisively to speak for those who were suffering from the actions of wrong-thinking bureaucrats. I find incredible motivation in shaping government to increase liberty, not restrict it unnecessarily. I'm sure I could find enough work for a lifetime focusing on securing freedom for Americans.

Over the years, I've put in my time campaigning for candidates in local races. I've pounded the pavement, donated, and made phone calls. I've taken personal responsibility for years to make sure that Nevada has worthwhile representatives.

No matter what role I see opening up for myself regarding government in the future, I know that my love and respect for this country will always shape my choices. I want what I do to add to the long-term freedom and security of this nation. I want my grandkids to be proud of the country that we all hand down to them. I want them to be able to say that we did our job taking good care of their inheritance.

And because that inheritance is such a powerful engine of liberty, we need to acknowledge our government's flaws without getting mired down in despair.

We need to temper clarity with hope so that we remain strong and able to do the work of democracy. I will always find motivation in working to maintain American integrity and justice.

36 | Sports

Let me ask you a question. Is something only worth doing if it brings you the big bucks?

I wonder about that question. Not for myself—I'm really clear on what is worthwhile to me and why. I just wonder about most people and the choices they make. I wonder what place sports holds for most of us, and why we place the importance on it that we do.

I see it especially in kids. In a lot of places, grownups are doing some weird things with kids' sports, going to one of two extremes. Either they want no competition or they want to treat kids like tiny pros.

Neither one is good for kids. We all played sports when we were growing up. Even if you never put on a uniform or joined a team, you played games with neighborhood kids or classmates at recess. And those games taught you a lot of valuable lessons.

You learned to work with a team. You learned to follow rules. And you learned that it's a lot more fun to win than to lose! These are basic social skills that kids need to learn on their own.

When we take the competitive element away, we're robbing kids of the joy of achievement and the thrill of contending for a prize. No wonder they lose interest if they get nothing for winning.

On the other hand, when adults let their egos take charge and make sports a deadly serious business, they remove the fun. They say to kids that sports are only worthwhile if you rise to the top of your field. Unless you make it to the pro level, none of your effort matters. I don't believe that.

As someone who did rise to the top of my field, I can see a lot of other benefits I got from boxing besides money, power, and fame. Winning titles and being on television were not what made boxing worthwhile to me. I got much more from pursuing this discipline than you would see at first. Here's what motivates me.

First, and most important, boxing unified my mind and body. For years, throughout my childhood, my mind had been at war with my body. My brain raced too fast, and it wouldn't let my body be still. Movement got treated like a character issue, like I had to confine and limit myself to act like all the other kids.

When I found boxing, I found the key to harnessing the incredible power of my mind. Sports worked to calm the mental racing I always sensed, making my mind and body a team instead of adversaries. To this day, if I need to consider a tough problem, come up with a creative approach, or commit some information to memory, I know that a run is my best tool.

Another benefit I got from boxing was health. If I had not found boxing, I might have ended up with a gut and some heart problems. With my natural love of great food, I might have overindulged. If I had not learned to exercise to make myself feel good physically, I might have turned to food for comfort instead.

So not only did exercise help me dodge a coronary bullet, it also gave me some great benefits. I've always had good numbers for weight, cholesterol, blood pressure, and blood sugar. I feel good in my body even now that I'm into my forties. I expect to feel good into my seventies. I won't age in the same way as people do who don't care for their bodies. So that's a definite benefit.

Comradeship is another benefit. I met people in the boxing world who have remained close friends for years, sometimes for decades. Boxing gave me Zook and Lenroy, guys I met in a gym in Florida who helped me see the influence I could have on others. Zook tells me that he learned to diversify income streams and pursue life wholeheartedly from me. Lenroy tells me that he learned persistence and dedication from me.

The world of boxing made me both a mentor and a student. From my coaches and mentors, I learned to take criticism and work hard. From those who looked to me, I learned the value of leading through personal excellence. By setting a good example, I had to say less. That was a valuable lesson that I carried into parenting.

I'm training my Dolly girl to see sports as recreation, as bonding time, as a thinking aid, and an investment in her future self. I want her to know about this great aid to mental and physical health much earlier than I did. That's why we go skiing and hiking and swimming when we spend time together.

Sports are such a huge part of my life that I can't imagine existing without them. It saddens me to hear about schools taking away PE and recess, especially knowing how busy kids can be after school. I worry that the coming generation isn't learning the intrinsic value of sports as a natural element of being human. They're seeing sports as an elite field where few will succeed and the rest are irrelevant. Let's bring back sports for all. Let's bring back athletes for life.

PART 5

POSITIVITY

> The only way to achieve success is by believing you can achieve your goals, no matter what. The story you tell yourself has the power to transform your life or destroy it. When you change your story, you can change your life.

TONY ROBBINS

37 | **Authenticity**

A huge part of being positive for me is authenticity. I don't have any secrets. There are no skeletons in my closet rattling the doorknob to get out. If you have finished reading this book, congratulations. You know me just about as well as anyone does.

It's important for me to live this way, out in the open, for a lot of different reasons. You know they say that if you don't lie, you don't have to have a good memory. (Take it from a skilled attorney; that's true!) Well, if you don't hide your past, you don't have to watch your back.

I wonder sometimes about all the potential out there that could benefit this country. I wonder how much of it gets hidden by people laying low because they want to hide their worst moments. That's really sad to me.

Look, we all have a learning continuum. Aristotle wasn't one of the world's most powerful minds when he was born. Abraham Lincoln wasn't the Great Emancipator when he was some scrawny backwoods kid. Muhammad Ali didn't seize his full power and greatness until he was well into adulthood.

We all have personal journeys. People mature at different levels. I made choices along the way with the maturity level and information I had at the time. I don't think I really grew up to the level I recognize now until after I turned forty.

If I had it to do over again, I would make different choices in some situations. But I can look at that younger Joey Gilbert and say, "Thanks, man. If you hadn't messed up, I wouldn't be where I am now."

I mean that. Every error is an opportunity to learn. Don't hide those growth opportunities. People need to know your story.

Here's one time I messed up that not a lot of people know. (I guess they do now!) But it changed the care I take with details.

During one of my long drives from Reno to Big Bear for training, I was pulled over. I didn't realize until later that I'd had a gun in the car, and I wasn't supposed to carry it across state lines. I felt especially stupid about it because I had just talked to Dad, who asked me whether I still had a gun in the car and then told me to take it out.

The gun didn't come up when I was pulled over, and as I couldn't do anything about it until I got back home, I stuck it into the inside pocket of my Toomey bag to deal with when I got home. Then I forgot about it.

Fast forward four months. I'm flying out of Anaheim back to Reno with one piece of luggage: my Toomey bag. The TSA stopped me and pulled me out of line. My first thought was, "Dang, I forgot to take my cologne out of the bag!"

I wasn't getting stopped for cologne.

Nope. For cologne they don't handcuff you in full sight of everybody else going through security. For a Glock 350, yep, they will lock you down. I was picture fodder for everyone heading through security that day who recognized me. That day was not one when I wanted to be recognized.

A huge sergeant walked over to deal with me and saw the cell phones popping. He looked me up and down. "You famous?"

"Yeah," I said. "I'm a fighter."

"Okay, let me see what I can do for you."

He went away and came back with a compromise while people in his office were talking. He couldn't get me out of handcuffs, but he let me sit down with a shirt over them. At least that stopped the improvised paparazzi. But then he heard back from his office.

"I've got to take you in."

"I understand, but I have a permit for this gun."

"We'll call over to Washoe County to confirm that. You understand we can't just take your word for it. And permit or not, it shouldn't have been crossing state lines or on an airplane in your carry-on."

"I will never forget that again!"

Funny how eight hours in jail, a second round of negative publicity, and a missed flight will drive a lesson home to you. I never did forget any element of gun safety or ownership after that day. The entire matter became much more present to me. In that area, I matured deliberately and significantly.

Now my records were sealed in that case. We could skip it, and you would never know. I have only one reason to put the whole story out in a book where I'm telling the reader (hi, there) that I have some important answers. Want to know that one reason?

Lies are toxic. As I mentioned before, I stay away from anything toxic. I don't want anything polluting my soul any more than I want anything polluting my body.

I don't drink, take drugs, or pop pills. I used to hit vapes until a friend questioned why I was messing with them when I was so healthy otherwise. Didn't I think they could be addictive? After that conversation, I put them down and haven't touched them since.

A big barrier to claiming champion status inside your own heart and working for what you want like you deserve to achieve it is that little voice inside telling you to hide. You need to shut that voice up by any means necessary. And if those means include radical honesty with everyone who matters to you about the ways you have messed up in the past, then do it.

I have a friend who caught his little brother breaking a rule when the brother was super little. So the friend was enough of a little shit that he held that broken rule over his little brother for years to get extra dessert or get out of chores or get the top bunk. The little brother was basically screwed because he didn't want his parents to know he'd messed up.

Then one day, my friend pulled out the old I-know-what-you-did line. His little brother looked him straight in the eye and said, "Go ahead and tell."

That's all it took to break the spell. He was free. He finally figured out that whatever punishment his parents gave him was going to be less painful than the price of that secret.

Guys: don't let anyone hold your past against you. Get in front of it. Get over it. Get it out there. Live out loud, and own your champion status.

If you're always thinking about your past mistakes, you won't be able to reach for any future greatness.

38 | Core Self

Here's another way to stay positive: make peace with your core self.

For me, that means acknowledging some qualities that others may perceive as negative. But I don't need to worry about what anyone else thinks. I worry about reality.

Take the ADHD diagnosis. A lot of people may consider that condition a detriment. I don't. I understand the ways it helps me perceive in the world and flow through my life, and I choose to take the way my mind works as a help to me.

For instance, I have an almost supernatural ability to cut through red tape. Other people look at a problem through an entire labyrinth of required process. I don't see the process as a necessary evil. I see it as an unnecessary obstacle, and I start looking for ways to obliterate it. If someone shows me a labyrinth, I will start busting down walls.

This made me a terrible airman in the National Guard. In the military, if there's steps 1-1000, you have to do them and do them in order. They think that you don't need explanations, you just need to follow orders.

But I realized a major way out of that labyrinth. I need to be in charge wherever I spend my time. It's an incredible relief to hand the duty of following orders to people I employ. And I enjoy rewarding them for initiative and efficiency.

I have surrounded myself over time with a team that knows how to take my constant flow of ideas and orders and run with it in the best possible way. They know that I can slow down and answer questions, but I don't need to spend forty minutes talking about why I want something done. They trust that I have good reasons for my orders, and they act as my extensions to follow through in ways I don't have the patience to pursue. Thank God for them.

I can get all stirred up and say in a verbal whirlwind what I'm going to do. I talk fast and leave it to other people to decode. That's why the people around me are so important, and trust me: I know how important they are. I know that one big weakness of mine is to assume that other people know what I'm talking about or why I want something done, while I'm thinking, "Just fucking do it, and know there's a reason why."

Because I understand how I work in the world, I've created this synergy that works for me and the people around me. The way my mind works, I also can keep track of a lot at once. Out of the blue, I can call on staff members with detailed expectations of work they were supposed to do.

I can say, "Hey, did you get this done?" and if the answer is yes, I'm the first one there with a high five.

If I have to remind staff of single duties, they'll turn to someone else and say, "How does he remember all that?"

Usually the answer is, "Worry about yourself. Let him worry about him."

Man, if I had fifty staff members, I could just destroy shit. If I had thousands, I could run the world!

A lot of times, people who get elected have no leadership skills. They may have great intelligence or great vision, but they can't manage people. But I know my weaknesses. I know what I don't know, and I love bringing smart people over and using them. I think that makes me a great leader.

I also realize that I need extra time to absorb and organize information. So I make sure that I am always prepared. I'm always taking the time well in advance to make sure that I do right by my clients and my partners.

And speaking of my clients and my partners, as well as my family, another part of my core self is my fierce love and protectiveness. I can't stand to see injustice, manipulation, or cruelty towards someone who is too weak or too nice to put up a strong defense. As far as I'm concerned, that's why I'm there.

At Joey Gilbert Law, the customer is not always right. The fact that you are going to cut me a check does not give you an automatic pass. I'm highly sensitive to the way people treat my team. So if I hear some client talking down to a person on my staff, that client is gone. We'll settle up the money, and that client can find some other attorney to put up with abuse and attitude, because that attorney is not me.

In the same vein, I won't defend third-time domestic offenders. The first time around, I figure maybe there was a loss of temper, an out-of-character moment that a client can regret, and every client deserves a fair defense under the law. I can get on board with that. The second time around, maybe there's an unhealthy relationship that needs some work. By the third time (and I'm well aware that it's just the third reported time), I'm seeing a pattern I can't defend. I'm seeing a bully, and my conscience will not allow me to support a bully.

I have told potential clients who thought they were above the law and above any common expectation of human decency that they had five minutes to leave my office before I beat their asses. One perk of name recognition for me is that I don't have to raise my voice for those clients to believe me and hightail it out of there.

The same thing goes for gang bangers. Believe me, I understand extenuating circumstances of life in low-income neighborhoods. Remember that GANGSTER speech? I can bend my mind around some empathy for hard situations. But by the time a client's lifestyle erases his own empathy for other people, I'm done. I'm much more motivated to defend the little guy, the guy who made one mistake, or the guy who has committed to turn things around for himself.

Understanding what lies at the core of me helps me

to view my life in a positive light. I know who I am, and I know what I bring to the world. I know how I work effectively and how to set myself up for success. That depth of self-knowledge is incredibly empowering and motivating.

39 | Gratitude

This story means a lot to me because it taught me about what it means to make a real connection with other people. It taught me about how I could speak into another person's life by listening carefully first. And like most good ideas I've had, it came to me on a run.

Like I said, I admired Tony Robbins so much that I went to every event I could manage. I attended one speaker boot camp where, in addition to instruction from Tony himself (one of the world's greatest speakers alive), we got to learn from Joe Williams. He was the lead speaker and head trainer for Tony, and he was super intense. The group Joe and Tony mentored consisted of about thirty-five people who would be together for the five days of the event.

I was motivated to do well in speaking because I had a nonprofit just sitting there. I'd set it up to use sports to help at-risk kids gain qualities that could help them succeed: direction, motivation, and self-confidence. I wanted to get on board with the speaker's bureau and get more going with the nonprofit in that way. If I could get booked as a speaker, I could draw more attention to the kids.

Because I was determined to wring every bit of benefit I could from these talented men at the top of their game, I volunteered for everything. You want someone to go first? Pick me! I'll go first every time.

Literally, Joe would give his students two minutes to prepare what to say, and I'd prepare. Then he'd ask, "Who's ready?" My hand shot up every time.

At the end of the course, we were going to give a longer speech that would be filmed. We'd have a day to prepare it, and then we'd be expected to show all that we had learned in all the days of instruction before. I knew that I wanted to pick a controversial topic to stir interest, one that lent itself to a memorable acronym, and I knew that I got my best ideas in motion. So I went on a run.

My mind wandered over all the controversial topics I'd encountered in my work, and suddenly, I hit on the word gangster almost at the same time that I hit on the first part of its acronym: get active now. I got the chill down my spine that let me know I was onto something.

Soon I had the rest of the acronym. I would argue that like everyone, gangsters had something positive to teach us, something we could learn by examining their name. Gangster could stand for Get Active Now, Generate Strategic Thought, Expect Results.

I knew that my middle class to wealthy classmates had one definite view of gangsters. I also knew that my acronym did not fit it. I wanted to irritate them and make them think, and that's exactly what my speech did. I filed away my success, left the Robbins event with some great speaking tools under my belt, and didn't think about GANGSTER for a while.

Then the people at Rite of Passage asked me to speak at one of their graduation events. They did the same work that my own nonprofit was doing, and I fully supported their efforts with youth. When they reached out, I knew that the time had come to dust off my thoughts about GANGSTER.

But I wasn't speaking to wealthy and middle-class entrepreneurs this time, and I definitely didn't want to irritate anyone. I knew that I needed to consider my audience and really put some thought into how some of these kids might view real gangsters. To some of them, GANGSTERs wouldn't be characters on TV or a defendant in a courtroom. They would be brothers, fathers, and friends. They might be terrifying presences. They would most certainly be real people.

After all, every single one of these kids had seen some shit; that's why they were there at ROP. I needed to take that reality into account. My speech would take on a whole new meaning.

So when I took the stage, I opened with a question. "Who knows what the word gangster means?"

I saw anxious looks dart between the teachers and puzzled ones appear on the faces of the kids. Where was this going?

"I know you all have your own ideas. I'm about to show you something important; so I really want to know what the word gangster means to you."

Here are some of the responses I got: family, loyalty, criminal, bad people, tough guy, brotherhood, you do what it takes. The more positive traits came from the kids. The more negative ones came from the teachers. I knew that my message would land in a good place with the kids.

"Wow! I can see that this word means different things to different people. I think that the word GANGSTER can stand for action. Do gangsters sit around all day, or do they stay busy?"

The kids all knew the answer to that. Gangsters hustled.

"And do you think that GANGSTERS have a plan? Do they know what they want to accomplish?"

Heads nodded. They were all too familiar with the clear goals of the gangs around them.

"So when these GANGSTERS stay busy acting on their plans, do they think that what they want to do will happen, or are they just staying busy for the sake of staying busy? Do they expect results?"

Kids were excited now. I looked around the room and saw every eye on me. I had connected to something that they knew. And I wasn't speaking of the people in their culture with disrespect and disgust. I had acknowledged the bad side that their teachers saw, and now I was speaking to them about the things in these unintentional neighborhood role models that they could take to heart and use. I had lit a fire in their imaginations.

I talked for a while about how to be successful. I

talked about constant motion, goal writing, self-discipline, and ambition. And I know that the kids in that room heard those ideas so much more differently than they would have if I had not taken the time to think about them specifically, connect to them, and listen to their perspective.

I am optimistic for the next generation. I know that they face challenges that we didn't face at their age, but I know from working with them that they are creative, resilient, and full of potential. Kids are repositories of boundless energy that we can direct in useful ways to benefit this whole country if we will only invest in them.

Let me tell you what I see when I spend time with at-risk kids. It's the same thing I see in some of my middle-class and wealthy clients with drug charges and DUIs. I see kids with a great big, lonely hole in the middle of their psyches where a parent is supposed to be. I see kids filling that lonely hole with substance abuse, gaming, and trouble.

We can bitch about the ways kids are dealing with loneliness and isolation all we want. That's not too effective in my opinion. If we really want to make a difference in the massive, national problem, we need to do it one kid at a time. Start with your own family. Spend time there. Then widen your circle to include your kid's friends whose parents are unwilling or unable to spend the time to make a difference. One kid at a time, we can invest care and thought and resources into helping kids feel a little less lonely, a little less likely to search for numbness or connection in an un-savory place.

Maybe we can help kids Get Active Now, Generate Strategic Thought, and Expect Results instead of becoming gangsters themselves. I believe we can. I believe that there is a nation full of awesome kids just waiting for us to try.

40 | **Fatherhood** (*Part 4*)

As she got older, Aiella became my sidekick. She was a bundle of energy like her old man, and she got to love sports just like I did. She could hang with me at the gym, punching heavy bags with her little fists or jogging alongside me. She liked active daddy-daughter days, where we'd go hiking, skiing, or swimming. When she developed a love for tennis, I took lessons, too, so that we could share that interest together.

Aiella constantly redirects me to positivity. There's an important biological component to that outlook. Her whole life is ahead of her with so much possibility. Standing with her, focusing on her and becoming her ally in all the ways she could succeed—that puts me in the mindset of looking to the future. I'm looking out for her good, and doing what's good for her does me good, too.

Take Spanish, for instance. My little girl and I both developed an interest in Spanish around the same time. She was learning some from our housekeeper / nanny and some from her school. I picked up some around the house and started learning some more on my own. I learned enough tourist-level words to communicate basic information and to do some promo spots. Keeping up with my Dolly girl was good for business!

Being Aiella's dad has been good for some personal growth moments, too, as hard as those might have been. I was going along like a lot of dads thinking that I was giving both of my girls all that they needed from me. They were very well provided for in the house I'd bought when Molly needed a place to stay during her pregnancy. They had every necessity and a lot of luxuries. Aiella only had to mention an interest for me to say, "Hey, let's find a class or a tutor on that!"

But when Aiella was about seven, Molly put her foot down. She made me see how things were from her point of view. I got to sail in for the fun stuff, the activities and parties and outings, but I left her with a lot of the not-fun work: the laundry and cooking and picking up. I was skipping out on the daily grind. Picking up the slack was wearing Molly out.

That come-to-Jesus-moment made an impression on me. I'm not going to say that I was perfect when it comes to picking up my gym towels or getting dinner on the table. I didn't suddenly become Mr. Mom. What I will say is that I made more of an effort from that time on to show up for more of the hard parts. I tried to be homework dad and carpool dad in addition to skiing dad and party dad.

And that was good for me. Remember those daily habits? Here they are again:

41 | **Forward Motion**

TOUCHING BASE
Do One Thing to Better Yourself Every Day

INTENTIONAL INTENSITY
*Push the Pace, Stay in the Pocket,
and Keep Throwing Punches.*

Up to now, I'd used those daily habits to better my physical fitness, my law firm, and my various business pursuits. Those habits, good as they were, mainly benefited me. They only brought benefit to those around me as an after effect.

Now I applied them to being Aiella's dad and a better help to Molly. I used the forward motion of the early morning hours to do one thing that would help them out, like getting Aiella ready for school, taking Aiella with me for a morning workout, or blending smoothies for breakfast. I'd try to take over one responsibility a day to make Molly's life easier and Aiella's life better. And when the daily grind got to be a grind, I took that lesson to heart about increasing intensity. This was something Molly did naturally. Moms just never quit when it comes to their kids. I took that intensity and determination for my own in regard to the less absorbing parts of parenting.

I needed that course correction to make it through the tough time that was coming. By the time Aiella was nine, it was clear to both Molly and me that we would not ever be a couple again. We were both pursuing relationships with other people. Molly moved to southern California, at first for a tennis camp with Aiella, but then she made her own life there.

The two of us eventually decided that Aiella would keep her home base here in Reno, and Molly would fly back and forth to see her. The separation was hard on Molly, and I could tell that Aiella was missing her mother. It was a tough time for all of us, a tough time that required more of me as a person, a man, and a father.

I went from being the dad who was trying to take on more of the daily tasks to the dad who was doing all of the tasks. Sure, I hired help. I kept a housekeeper, and I hired tutors and coaches as part of the parenting team I supervised to keep Aiella moving forward. But I was on point all day every day.

For the last few years, I've slowed down for my little girl. I've learned to take a step down when I need to spend time with her. I've invested more than I thought possible when she was an infant and I was wrestling with becoming a father.

Now my day centers around my daughter. Things are turned upside down with Covid-19 restrictions, anyway, and so I've used those requirements to remake my home around Aiella. I've installed lights for Zoom both for her lessons and my work. I work from home whenever I can. I've brought kids into the house to simulate class for her. I've hired the top female Brazilian fighter in the world to teach her Jiu Jitsu. Sly Stallone summed up my feelings on fatherhood when he said that you do whatever it takes for your kid. Yes, you do.

That time together has paid off so far. Aiella has been traveling with me since she was seven or eight years old. Now she can book flights, order food, and book hotels. This girl is eleven going on eighteen! She's eager, ambitious, daring, and curious. She's bold and adventurous.

That's a kind of redemption for me. I still have a wound inside from leaving Chicago when I was young. I have always felt that was a way my parents failed me, introducing insecurity and pain where it didn't exist before. I like to think I took those feelings and used them to inform the way I made choices for Aiella. Kids are not as resilient as you think. You have to put them first where baseline security and happiness is concerned.

Fatherhood means that you become a stud and a leader. You make that kid the priority, and under no circumstances do you leave. After medical marijuana became legal in Nevada, I had so many opportunities to pursue the cannabis business in other states. I had almost unlimited funding available to fight for cannabis rights and open dispensaries in state after state, staying out a week and coming home for a week. But that wasn't best for my Dolly girl, and so I shut down those offers.

Getting Aiella to a place where she's comfortable and happy is everything to me. Making sure her best interests are served is the primary focus of my life now, no question. And I couldn't be happier to be making those choices.

So Dolly girl, if you are reading this right now, I want to talk straight to you. I know it was hard for you to read the other three sections about how I didn't want to be a daddy. I want you to know that when I thought those things, I didn't know you. I could never have imagined how much I would love you or how much you would mean to me. My imagination just wasn't that good.

So honey, I am glad beyond my ability to tell you that you are here. I wouldn't trade you for all the LA dreams in the world. You are the most precious person in the world to me. My life would be incomplete without you.

Thank you for being the ultimate gift of the universe to me.

42 | **Learning**

I'm sure I wasn't the student she expected. I took up a lot of space on that narrow bench, and the hands that spanned the lines of black and ivory were more suited to making fists than pressing keys. But here I was, with a beginner book leaning against the music stand, starting from scratch.

Why was I learning piano in my late thirties? I was well past the traditional start date. Usually students began piano because their mothers made them, and usually those students were in elementary school. Nobody was making me do anything. Nobody but me.

Christmas lights still shone on the tree in our spacious living room, reflecting off the glossy, black surface of the piano I'd bought for Aiella. But like most opportunities I brought her way, I didn't want her to approach it alone. If I was going to tell her that learning music would benefit her throughout her life, bringing her enjoyment and helping her think in new ways, then I was more than willing to sign up for those benefits, too.

Aiella is the reason for a lot of the new skills I try. I see her so open to life and so willing to find joy in new places, and she inspires me to invest time and attention in learning some new things, too. She's a big inspiration to me.

But learning offers me more than just a way to connect with my Dolly girl. Learning keeps me sharp, expands my mind and soul, and provides me plenty of opportunities for humility. It's a core value for me.

I know that the grey matter between my ears is going to age. Some things are out of your control. A disease like Parkinson's or Alzheimer's could rob me of the mental clarity I prize so highly as an attorney. But study after study shows that learning new things helps stave off the cognitive fuzziness that occurs with normal aging.

Look at it like exercise. You have to keep exercising the muscles in your body day after day. If you do, you'll see the reward of a strong, healthy body that can do what you want. I view learning in the same way. If I want my mind to perform at the level I expect, I need to make it work in new ways continually. With each new endeavor I embrace, I reinforce the old neural pathways and open new ones.

That's important—opening new neural pathways. I don't know of anything more discouraging than seeing someone set in his or her ways. To refuse to embrace another perspective, another set of experiences, not only limits people but sours them. Do you know someone like this? You can identify the narrow thinkers in your family and social circle by listening for complaints. Those who complain the most focus only on set expectations and how things out there are failing to meet those expectations.

Forget that! Where's the creative thinking? Where's the problem solving? Where's the positivity and hope and curiosity that are the only qualities that ever fixed things? No one in the history of the world has made life better by sitting on the sidelines and grumbling about how many idiots are screwing things up.

I refuse to play Statler and Waldorf—the critics in the balcony—in the Muppet Show of life. Why would you withdraw and harp on the chaos when you could go on stage and play? On stage is where the fun is: the singing, dancing, joking, and playing.

When you learn something new, you're opening your mind, yes, and you are also opening your soul. You're turning your capacity to appreciate life in a new direction and asking more of the world to bring you joy and wonder. Learning wakes you up to notice more.

It's like watching the sun come up. First you notice the shapes of things, and then details start to appear. When the rays of light top the hills, they touch the earth with color where everything was grey before. The golds and reds and oranges bring out new dimensions in the browns and greens of the ground. If you only see the earth by the cold starlight of early dawn, how much you miss!

The good book says that a little child shall lead them, and I'm here to tell you that only the adults who can embrace life with the passion, openness, and humility of childhood will ever sustain old age with dignity.

Humility. I can almost hear some of you smirking

that I sure could use a dose of that! Ha! Don't worry. I'm getting my fair share.

Because I value learning for itself, I regularly put myself in a position where I don't know anything, where I'm not the smartest guy in the room. Then I find someone smarter than me and ask questions. I follow directions. I practice.

A lot of times, I can look foolish starting at the beginning of something. Take tennis. As a boxer, I've trained my body to move with certain reflexes. My arms anticipate angles of motion and degrees of pressure appropriate to causing harm to my opponent.

In tennis, I have to learn to balance effort with restraint. My arms have to fine-tune their motor skills, just like my mind has to calculate force and tension in all kinds of new ways. I make mistakes sometimes. I can trip and fall down, as I have, and I can miss the ball with a wild swing, as I have. According to Aiella, that looks pretty goofy.

But I have a lot of fun, and I don't take myself too seriously. I can play. I'm not here to win the Grand Slam but to enjoy a new activity and change the way I move and think. And I spend time with my favorite child, which is just gravy.

Here's another for-instance: Spanish. Maybe you remember the high-school embarrassment of trying to wrap your tongue and teeth around the rolled r sounds, nasal n sounds, and new pronunciations of a vocabulary you struggled to remember. I bet you also remember some ratty teenager making fun of you for trying. Am I right?

You're going to feel foolish sometimes when you do things wrong. That's okay. It's not the end of the world.

I really feel that we introduce language at the worst time in our educational system. Kids should learn languages early, when they're not too proud or insecure to make weird sounds with their mouths. Ever been in an elementary school cafeteria? That's what the kids do for fun! Have them imitate the phonetic sounds in French or Spanish or Chinese while they want to do it and while their minds are drinking up facts like a sponge. That's the time to absorb vocabulary.

As an adult learning a new language, you have to tap into that elementary-school fearlessness. You've got to make peace with the possibility of sounding a little strange to yourself and the other people in the room. Trust me. It's good for you.

Destroy the limiting belief that you have to be as good as a professional for your effort to be worthwhile. The point is not to outdo Itzhak Perlman or Yehudi Menuhin. The point is to make your brain translate written music into sound, to feel the pressure of the string under your finger, and to smell the rosin and wood of the violin. The point is also to appreciate the incredible investment of life it takes to become a genius like those men did. The point might also be to hear music in a different way, from the perspective of a participant instead of just a consumer. And the point is also to enjoy the making of melody.

We grow or we die, right? Challenge yourself to grow.

Humble yourself to ask questions and really listen to the answers. Appreciate the gifts in the people around you. Grow into someone who can adapt to whatever life brings you.

See you in the nursing home, Champ. I'll be the one at the piano belting out La Bamba and waiting for painting lessons to start. As long as I draw breath, there will be something new for me to learn.

43 | Joy

A lot of circumstances in my life as I've grown have been hard. And it seems sometimes that the more I grow, the harder things get. It's not all my inviting it with my take-charge attitude and in-your-face approach to life, either. Some things are just hard.

The entire year of 2020 was hard in ways I never anticipated. For an extrovert like me, curtailing social interaction was hard. You don't like to admit that isolation is getting you down, but if you don't acknowledge it, you can't fight it.

Seeing the country change and lose its heart and its way was tough, too. I have hope that we will recover and remember who we are before we lose too much of ourselves. But I've channeled a lot of anger, frustration, and despair into my heavy bag and my running shoes this year.

Over the past year, I have also been dealing with some fallout from the end of my relationship with Molly. There have been hurt feelings and unmet expectations that we have both had to address like grownups for the sake of our much-loved daughter. As the custodial parent over the last year, I've been the main source of comfort and stability for a little person whose life

223

looks a lot different than it has in the past.

Maybe you've been dealing with a lot over the last year, too. Maybe you feel hopeless some days. You know in your head what it takes to be a champ, but depending on the day, you may or may not follow through with the actions that will make you one. Some days, positivity may feel like a pipe dream.

When I feel like that, I turn to my earliest source of advice and well-being: my faith. I connect to that source of ultimate goodness and remember the words of St. Julian of Norwich. "All shall be well, and all shall be well, and all manner of thing shall be well."

It's true. Darkness and light come in cycles, like morning following midnight. And in the times when we can't see our way forward, it is our job to believe that there is one, and if we just keep walking until the light appears, we'll see it.

That's what joy feels like to me. It's this assurance deep inside that the world will make sense again one day and that all the footsteps I take in the dark will lead me to a good place. It's this knowledge that God wastes nothing.

With this decision to act in joy, I can bring a little of the future light into my present, no matter what's happening. I can put a little distance between me and my feelings, knowing that they're not ultimate reality. Joy keeps me going.

Joy is such an important element of positivity. You can't just gin up this feeling 24/7. It's too much to expect any person to do. That's why you need some kind of an outside force. You need to know, deep inside, that God is for you, or that the universe is on your side. You need to be able to draw on that knowledge and tell yourself that all manner of thing shall be well—not because you will it to be well but because God does.

You remember when I missed that deadline for the bar exam and Justice Michael Douglas took that petition for my retake around to the other judges? I had put in all the work and effort to study for the bar exam. I was going to be the one to take it. But I had a powerful ally on my side working for me to have the opportunity to shine.

That's a good image for me of the balance of work and faith that resolves into joy. I keep pressing hard for what I believe I should do and what I want to do, and I know that God is working for the very same thing. Even when I can't see it. Especially when I can't see it.

44 | Choice

When I lived in Chicago as a small child, my heroes were gangsters—wise guys. I liked that spunk and independence from what anyone told them to do and that determination to make a buck by any means available. I modeled myself on that opportunistic, daring, adventurous bunch of guys that had each other's back. After all, they weren't working just for themselves— they were working for a family.

Then I got here to Nevada, where the regional heroes were a little different, but a lot the same. Both had the same fire and ingenuity and drive to succeed. But now I was in the Silver State, named for the metal that miners pulled from the ground. Those miners were the heroes here.

These guys were out entirely for themselves. They'd migrated from out east drawn by dreams of gold and glory. And that migration was a definite risk. Many people didn't make it. Considering the potential dangers of slow starvation, wild animals, serious disease, fatal injury, and exposure to extreme conditions, they didn't make the decision to travel west lightly.

Leaving home was hard for them. There were no phone lines, and there wouldn't be a transcontinental railroad for decades. The Pony Express, despite its excellent reputation, was often a crapshoot, and the other method of transporting mail was by steamship rounding the southern coast and offloading bags to a train that crossed Panama to another steamship going up the coast to California. Either way, they likely wouldn't hear from their families for months, if not years.

But the reward was unimaginable wealth. A man with enough luck might work a year or two and return with more money than he could have earned in ten lifetimes. Enough courage and optimism and pigheadedness could yield a lifetime of prosperity and ease. For thousands of young Americans, that trade seemed like a good deal.

It didn't work out for everyone—not by a long shot. I've often thought that Nevada was peopled by those who never gave up trying. Those who tried and failed and kept trying passed the dream along to their descendants. They didn't go back east because they hadn't yet arm-wrestled fate to the ground and taken their winnings. But by God, they would.

Doesn't it make sense that Nevada would become the home of American gambling? Where else could the casinos of Las Vegas and Reno have possibly found a home but here? There's a collective memory of risk that informs the direction of commerce in this state.

I look around Nevada, and I see the sons and daughters of the miners, the pioneers. Adventure is in their blood. They understand taking chances.

That's a kind of positivity, too. You are willing to take risks only when you believe in yourself and value adventure. Taking chances means that you embrace the future and all it will bring you.

It also requires a sense of fun and curiosity. Adventure is almost a kind of play, and it's oddly more likely to pay off when you can approach it that way. Energy draws like energy, after all.

One of the things I hated most about Covid was the way it sapped the will of the nation to do something, anything, to make things better. People didn't try new things. They didn't dare to act. They were told to stay home and sit on their hands, and for the most part, that's what they did.

Not everyone. I saw people start new businesses, devote time and energy to new skills and pursuits. Some people capitalized on opportunity and grew as human beings.

Inaction and fear are the opposite of a champion's mindset. A champion doesn't stand at a fork in the road indefinitely, afraid to travel down either path. A champion moves forward boldly and cheerfully, willing to take the consequences or accept the rewards for his or her choices.

You know, I've learned a lot from Nevada miners— and not just in principle. My buddy Clint gave me a book about ten years ago written by a historian who grew up in a little Nevada town in the early 1900s. She would visit her grandfather, one of the pioneer miners from the century before, and listen to his stories about claim jumpers, explosions, back-breaking work, and fortunes in the ground.

This book she wrote in the 1950s preserved all that history in a way that fascinated me. And you know me—when something fascinates me, the business wheels in my brain start turning. I saw with new eyes that mining wasn't just Nevada's history. It could be the future.

It was definitely the present. Over eighty percent of the gold in the United States comes from Nevada, which is still a leader in mining. Clint, who grew up around Virginia City, had gold fever a couple of times in his life. Lucky for me, it was catching.

I read that book on my way to a beach somewhere for Christmas in 2011, and by the time I arrived on vacation, my gold fever was burning hot. I called Clint from the beach and told him, "We've got to own a mine."

Through some family connections (that sound gangster enough for you?) I heard about a promising one that could yield profits from metals and water rights. Currently, the owners were battling some bad actors who were running a scam selling shares to investors when they didn't even own the land.

I wasn't taking any chances. The law is a big and complicated field with many specialties, one of which is mining law. In 2012, I hired a mining attorney, opened a company, and purchased the land rights. I got my Dad involved as an initial investor along with the mining attorney. Then the court cases started coming with the bad actors. We had to get them out once and for all so that we could start capitalizing on our investment. We didn't want to hoodwink other people into giving us money to develop the mine's potential without doing anything for real. We actually wanted to bring treasure out of the ground, just like the old guys before the Civil War.

A few years later, we brought Clint in as a partner in that company. So far, we've both poured hundreds of thousands of dollars and a hell of a lot of sweat equity into our mining venture. We've won eight out of nine lawsuits. The fight isn't over yet, but one day, it will be. When that day comes, the profit may reach $50 million, though it won't be less than $20 million.

That's plutocracy money. That's money that will buy you a seat at the table for any conversation you feel is worth having. And boy, do I feel like having a whole lot of conversations with a whole lot of powerful people.

I know I'm taking a risk. Hey, the courts may decide against me one day, though I very highly doubt it. The risk I'm taking is less like a slot machine and more like a poker game where I know I've got a winning hand. But I may be pouring a sizeable investment straight into the dry Nevada soil.

You know what? That's a risk I'm willing to take in light of the information I have and the potential reward for seizing my moment. I see a way to win, and I have the stones to stake my claim. I dare. I triple-dog dare, and I'm not backing down.

Take a lesson from the miners of my adopted home state. Find out what dream is so appealing to you that you'd risk it all to get it. Then take that risk. Climb aboard that wagon. Toss those dice. Step onto that path. You can be a champion.

The choice is yours.

45 | Life Lessons

Did you ever try to find the pot of gold at the end of a rainbow when you were a kid? I did. I'd heard that legend that leprechauns hid their treasures at the rainbow's end, and if you could find it, you could have it. I remember noting the exact spot over a neighbor's house where that rainbow touched down and running excitedly over backyards to reach it. When I got there, I saw that the end of the rainbow had somehow moved while I was running.

When I grew older and learned what rainbows really were and realized that they had no end, I learned the lesson of the legend. You can't just chase the hope of a big windfall you didn't earn. It's a waste of time. Leprechauns are sneaky little bastards.

I feel like summing up all the lessons of my life is kind of like chasing a rainbow's end. That's a moving target because I'm not done learning them myself. I still have quite a few neighbors' yards to cross. This book written at this fairly early (knock wood) point in my life isn't the book I'll write at eighty or at ninety.

Still, looking back to where I started, I feel that I do have some lessons under my belt that I can share. So keep in mind that I'm sharing an unfinished journey.

Here are the signposts I've passed so far.

The first is the importance of family. Whether it was through the heartbreak of leaving my close community in Chicago, the shock of learning my parentage, or the assurance of turning to Poppy Aiello or my sister Gina for comfort, I grew to understand at a heart level that family is primary. The addition of my own daughter only underscored that fact for me.

Aiella also gave me a direction for that lesson, an action step. I can choose today to rewrite my family story. I can take the good parts of my family and use them to benefit the next generation. So I see in my leadership Warren Gilbert's strength of character. I can see in my stability Poppy Aiello's warmth. I can see in my daily presence the longing I had for an absent father and the connection I have with a present one. Aiella benefits now and in the future because of that lesson in family I learned in the past.

I also learned the lesson of resilience. Boy, did I get knocked down as a kid! The move to Nevada knocked down my sense of identity and security. The bullies I faced knocked down my pride and my physical body. And then I faced some tough blows as a grownup: failing the bar, withstanding false accusations, and deferring my dreams.

But each time I got knocked down, I got back up. I learned that I wasn't the guy who suffered a gut punch. I was the guy who got back up and raised his fists, ready for the next round. I wasn't a victim. I was a champion.

Resilience meant persisting in the next good, right thing to do. It meant trying again when it looked like my chances were up. It meant letting the bad opinions of other people about me slide off me while I turned to my good humor and perseverance. It meant finding another way to succeed when the way I'd chosen didn't work out.

Another lesson I learned was the value of optimism. Where would I have been today if I let hard things make me bitter to the world? I wouldn't be successful, healthy, and happy. I know that for sure.

Some of the biggest successes I've had have come from positive curiosity about the world. I truly believe that good things are out there, just waiting to happen. Because of that belief, I'm alive to the possibilities that present themselves.

Have you ever taken a romantic, horse-drawn carriage ride or seen one go by? I just can't bring myself to think of them as romantic when I consider the horses. They wear blinkers, panels to the side of their eyes, so that they can only see the road ahead of them, and in most large cities they wear a poop bag to keep the streets clean. But what kind of existence is that, walking in pointless circles where everything is the same and dragging your shit behind you?

I refuse to live like a carriage horse. I'm a stallion, baby! I run where the hell I want and leave the shit in my past far behind me. See a fence in my way? Good thing I can jump!

Here's the final signpost on my path: determination.

I know that only daily work will get me to my goals. That's why I believe in no days off. You keep fighting and fighting until you win.

Every day, you get up and do what needs to be done for that day. You don't let feeling tired or listening to discouragement stop you. You just get shit done. You tell yourself that it will matter, that it will make all the difference in the end. And if you tell yourself that enough times, it becomes true.

When you become an adult on a journey, you stop expecting to find a pot of gold flashing light at you with a colorful come-and-get-it allure. You get your own pot and start making your own gold to go inside. You find that you already had a lot of gold inside to start with.

This is what I know. Keep your family close. Learn to get back up. Expect good of the world. And work your heart out. Follow those signposts through your own life, and you will make your own magic.

46 | Determination

Here's the point. Living in a continual reach for champion status takes willpower and discipline. That is it. That's the total key. You will never see anyone successful who doesn't have willpower.

I asked you right up front if you were a champion. I told you that you have to decide you're a champion before you can apply my championship formula. I stand by that statement, and after getting to know me in these pages, I hope you can see why I consider willpower the cornerstone of any success formula.

You don't walk into a boxing gym on a dare and get where I got and still carry that record without being disciplined. I continue to train every day, run every day, and work every day. I hang bags at my office just like I did in my frat house, and I take what moments I can to throw combinations.

You may have heard of the theory of greatness taught by Malcolm Gladwell in his book *Outliers*. Basically, you become an expert if you practice a skill consistently for ten thousand hours. I wanted to get through my ten thousand hours as fast as possible, and so I dedicated myself to practicing excellence.

236

As a result, I have a PhD in delegation and management. I have a PhD in success and results. I have trained myself in the art of compartmentalization to the point where I am able to get shit done to an astounding degree.

That PhD is the reason I know I can come to you with my honest story and tell you, "I know how you can become a champ." I do know. I know because I've done it.

We've gone through a lot of stories together about a lot of different things that have happened in my life. Along the way, I've shared some principles with you that I consider vital. The stories may explain how I got to the principles, but because you don't have my life or my circumstances, you can't recreate the conditions of my victories.

You should instead focus on the lessons I learned from them. And the most important lessons are the five areas of focus that will make you a CHAMP. Here they are again:

- COMMUNITY—*Surround yourself with winners and supporters. You don't have to limit yourself to the group nature handed you.*

- HEALTH—*You get to choose what to do with what you have. No matter where you're starting, you can make the most of it.*

- AMBITION—*That fire in the belly is up to you, too. No one else is going to make you want to win.*

- MOTIVATION—*What gets you excited? What matters to you? Focus your ambition on that.*

- POSITIVITY—*Believe that your dreams are within your reach. If you start out with a no inside, you won't be able to see all the yeses in the world.*

So that's *The Championship Formula.* Put your resources into developing those five areas, and you will see the benefit. How do you place your resources? You can work on developing each area every day with the three daily steps:

- Forward Motion. *Get Up and Get Moving*

- Touching Base. *Do One Thing to Better Yourself Every Day*

- Intentional Intensity: *Push the Pace, Stay in the Pocket, and Keep Throwing Punches.*

So every morning, execute those three steps. Focus on the five areas. And use the lessons I learned from boxing. Remember the boxing lessons that got me through law school?

- **Discipline and willpower.** *Be your own boss. Learn to give yourself instructions and follow them.*

- **Constant motion.** *Don't stop moving. No days off.*
- **Fists up.** *Do the hard work before you step into whatever ring you choose, and once you get there, protect yourself in practical ways.*

- **Fair play.** *Fight fair. Don't be a jackass.*

- **Perpetual vigilance.** *Look for opportunity, and believe you're going to find it.*

That's how you focus on the five areas of being a CHAMP. There are so many other lessons I really hope you gleaned from getting to know me. I'll note a few below:

- *Find good mentors. Learn from them.*
- *Stand on the strengths of your heritage.*
- *Plan your life, and then work that plan.*
- *Take your haters as a dare to win.*
- *Pay attention to the details.*
- *And most importantly, work your ass off.*

That last one means the most to me. If I could put this whole book into one short sentence, that would be it. Work your ass off. Nothing else matters without that element. Champions work. That's what I know.

It's been an honor to share my life and my perspective with you. If you're ever in trouble in Nevada, look me up. And if you become a CHAMP because of something I taught you, let me know.

Nothing would make me happier than for you to win at life.

About the Author

Joey Gilbert, a lawyer, former fighter, and entrepreneur, is also a father fighting for his daughter and the future of all children. For the past nineteen months, he has been fighting to take back our cities, counties, schools, and state. During his fight for citizen rights, Gilbert has gone toe to toe with the Nevada governor, whom he sued for access to the early treatment medication hydroxychloroquine. Gilbert also filed a lawsuit to free Nevada's churches from unlawful Covid restrictions, taking the governor to the ninth circuit court of appeals and beating him just in time to open all Nevada churches for Christmas in 2020.

Joey Gilbert's unique background stems from his time as a student athlete, Air Force Reservist via Individual Ready Reserve (IRR), professional prizefighter, and entrepreneur. A three-time National Champion Collegiate Boxer, four-time

Regional Champion, and four-time All-American, Gilbert became the Nevada Golden Gloves Super Middleweight Champion after returning from basic training for the Nevada Air National Guard in 2000.

While attending law school, he appeared on NBC's *The Contender* alongside Sylvester Stallone and Sugar Ray Leonard. Afterwards, he won two regional world title belts (WBO-NABO and WBC-USNBC); ranked #3 in the world within the World Boxing Organization (WBO); and placed #7 in the world in the World Boxing Council (WBC). In 2011, Gilbert chose to pursue his legal career and other business endeavors. He retired with 21 victories, 17 knockouts, and 3 defeats.

Opening his own law firm in 2009, Gilbert quickly earned success. In 2021, Joey Gilbert Law was named "Best Law Firm" and "Best Personal Injury Attorney" in Reno by the very liberal Reno Gazette Journal. He parlayed this success into public service, assisting Nevada's citizens in opening eight counties without Covid restrictions, helping three counties to become constitutional counties, and recently filing a lawsuit against the vaccine mandate in all Nevada universities and community colleges.

He is currently in federal court fighting the mask mandate on our children. He is Chairman of the Board of America's Frontline Doctors and serves as its Director of Strategy,. He is fighting alongside the most brilliant attorneys and doctors in the world on behalf of medical human rights.

CPSIA information can be obtained
at www.ICGtesting.com
Printed in the USA
LVHW091638170622
721548LV00014B/1045

9 781649 215475